W9-DDU-819

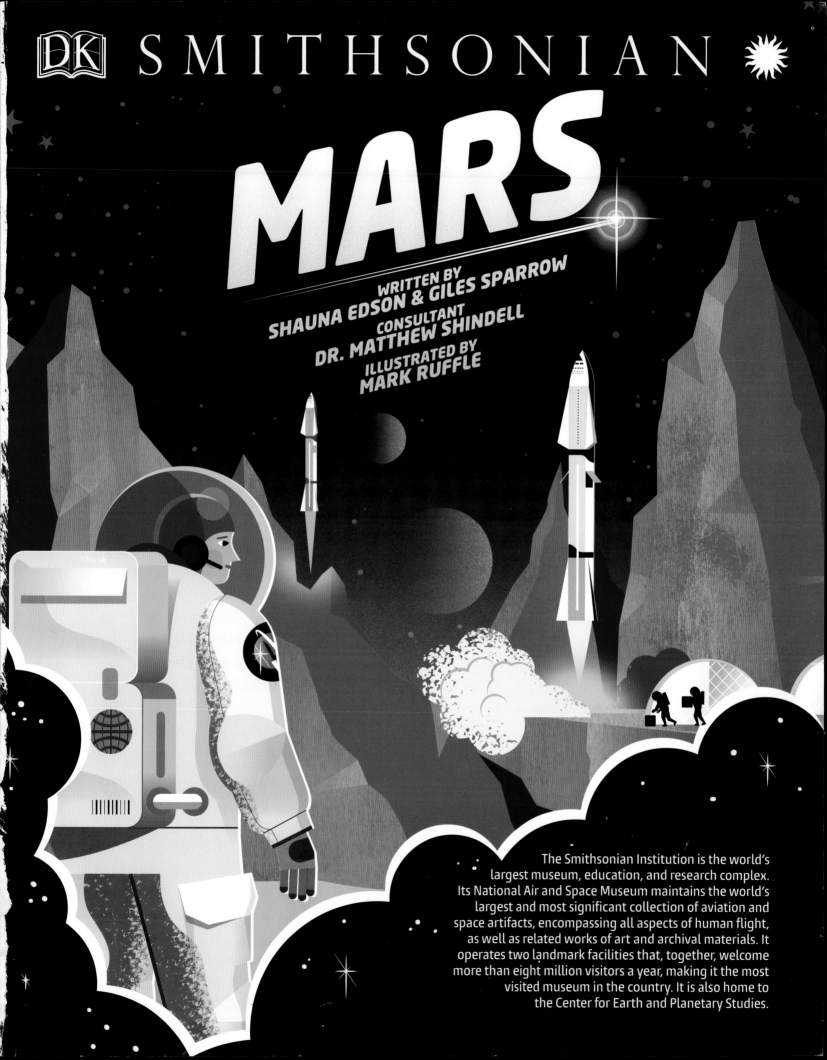

SMITHSONIAN

MARS

WRITTEN BY
SHAUNA EDSON & GILES SPARROW

CONSULTANT
DR. MATTHEW SHINDELL

ILLUSTRATED BY
MARK RUFFLE

The Smithsonian Institution is the world's largest museum, education, and research complex. Its National Air and Space Museum maintains the world's largest and most significant collection of aviation and space artifacts, encompassing all aspects of human flight, as well as related works of art and archival materials. It operates two landmark facilities that, together, welcome more than eight million visitors a year, making it the most visited museum in the country. It is also home to the Center for Earth and Planetary Studies.

Editor Sophie Parkes
Designer Sonny Flynn
Project Art Editor Charlotte Bull
US Senior Editor Shannon Beatty
US Editor Margaret Parrish
Jacket Coordinator Issy Walsh
Picture Researcher Nimesh Agrawal, Sakshi Saluja
Managing Editor Penny Smith
Managing Art Editor Mabel Chan
Senior Producer, Pre-Production Nikoleta Parasaki
Producer Inderjit Bhullar
Creative Director Clare Baggaley
Publishing Director Sarah Larter

Written by Shauna Edson and Giles Sparrow
Illustrated by Mark Ruffle
Consultant Dr. Matthew Shindell

First American Edition, 2020
Published in the United States by DK Publishing
1450 Broadway, Suite 801, New York, NY 10018

Copyright © 2020 Dorling Kindersley Limited
DK, a Division of Penguin Random House LLC
20 21 22 23 24 10 9 8 7 6 5 4 3 2 1
001–316418–Mar/2020

All rights reserved.
Without limiting the rights under the copyright reserved above, no part of this
publication may be reproduced, stored in or introduced into a retrieval system,
or transmitted, in any form, or by any means (electronic, mechanical,
photocopying, recording, or otherwise), without the prior written permission of
the copyright owner.
Published in Great Britain by Dorling Kindersley Limited

A catalog record for this book
is available from the Library of Congress.
ISBN 978-1-4654-8990-6

DK books are available at special discounts when purchased
in bulk for sales promotions, premiums, fund-raising, or educational use. For
details, contact: DK Publishing Special Markets,
1450 Broadway, Suite 801, New York, NY 10018
SpecialSales@dk.com

Printed and bound in China

A WORLD OF IDEAS:
SEE ALL THERE IS TO KNOW

www.dk.com

INTRODUCTION

PAST

PRESENT

FUTURE

CONTENTS

WELCOME TO MARS!

Mars is full of history and mysteries that we are learning more about all the time.

What is Mars like up close? Did it ever have life? How could we live there one day? In this book, we will answer these questions and more by exploring the past, present, and future of Mars. You will learn what we know about it now and will consider the many things we don't understand yet.

But before we begin, here are some useful things to know as you read about the amazing Red Planet.

USEFUL THINGS TO KNOW

PLANET

A planet is an object in space that moves around the sun. It is ball-shaped and can be made of rock, gas, metal, ice, or a mixture of these materials. There are eight known planets in our solar system.

MARTIAN

This describes anything concerning the planet Mars.

SOLAR SYSTEM

The solar system is the sun and everything that travels around it. This includes planets, moons, dwarf planets, and other objects. The solar system is one small part of the Milky Way galaxy, which is a huge collection of stars and other space objects.

ATMOSPHERE

Most planets are wrapped in a layer of air, called an atmosphere. A planet's gravity pulls the atmosphere close to it. Earth has an atmosphere made of nitrogen and oxygen gas, which we breathe every day. Mars also has an atmosphere; it is mostly made from carbon dioxide, and is much thinner than Earth's.

ROTATION

All the planets rotate, or spin. One rotation is what we call a day. On Earth, this takes 24 hours. Each planet rotates at a different speed, so one day on another planet can be longer or shorter than on Earth. One Mars day, which we call a "sol," is only about 37 minutes longer than an Earth day.

MASS

The amount of material that makes up an object.

GRAVITY

Objects are pulled toward other objects because of a force called gravity. How much gravity an object has depends on how much mass it has. It is a force that works even if two objects are not touching each other, but it is strongest when the objects are closest. The sun's gravity pulls on the planets and objects in the solar system, and the objects pull back, even though they are millions of miles apart.

ORBIT

An orbit is a path that an object in space takes around another, which repeats over and over again. An orbit is an oval shape. Mars and the other planets travel around the sun in orbits, and the sun's gravity holds them there. Some planets orbit closer to the sun than others — their distance from the sun affects how long they take to complete one orbit, which is called a revolution. On Earth, one revolution takes 365 days — this is why one year lasts this long. Mars is farther from the sun, so one revolution takes about 687 days.

NASA

This stands for the National Aeronautics and Space Administration. It is an organization created by the US government that is in charge of space exploration, developing technology and sending missions to space.

ESA

This stands for the European Space Agency. It is an organization created by governments from 22 countries in Europe, and it is dedicated to space exploration. It does research and plans many missions.

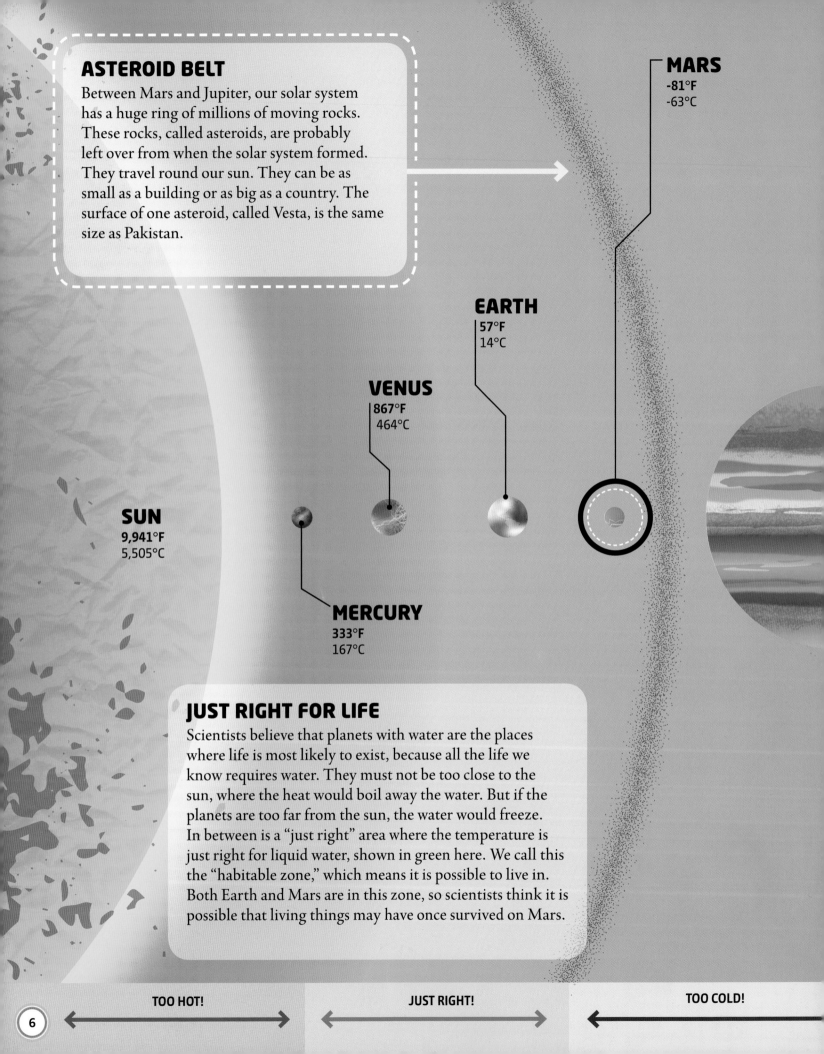

ASTEROID BELT

Between Mars and Jupiter, our solar system has a huge ring of millions of moving rocks. These rocks, called asteroids, are probably left over from when the solar system formed. They travel round our sun. They can be as small as a building or as big as a country. The surface of one asteroid, called Vesta, is the same size as Pakistan.

MARS
-81°F
-63°C

EARTH
57°F
14°C

VENUS
867°F
464°C

SUN
9,941°F
5,505°C

MERCURY
333°F
167°C

JUST RIGHT FOR LIFE

Scientists believe that planets with water are the places where life is most likely to exist, because all the life we know requires water. They must not be too close to the sun, where the heat would boil away the water. But if the planets are too far from the sun, the water would freeze. In between is a "just right" area where the temperature is just right for liquid water, shown in green here. We call this the "habitable zone," which means it is possible to live in. Both Earth and Mars are in this zone, so scientists think it is possible that living things may have once survived on Mars.

TOO HOT!

JUST RIGHT!

TOO COLD!

WHERE IS MARS?

Our solar system is made up of the sun and the planets, moons, and other objects that surround it. Mars is the fourth planet away from the sun. There are eight planets altogether.

Usually, the closer a planet is to the sun, the hotter it is at its surface. Imagine standing near a campfire on a cold day — the closer to the fire you stand, the warmer you feel. Earth and Mars are at the right distance for their surfaces to be neither too hot nor too cold. The planets farther away from the sun are much colder.

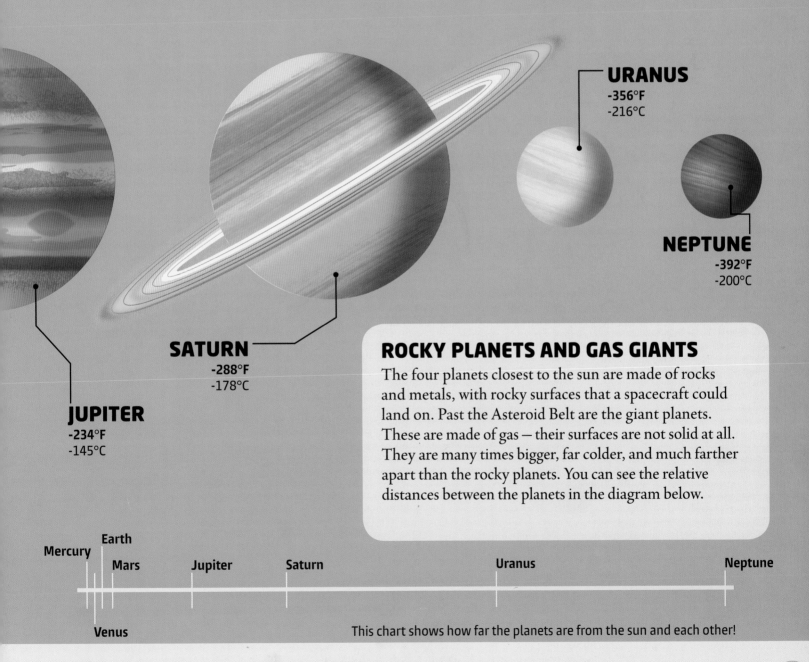

URANUS
-356°F
-216°C

NEPTUNE
-392°F
-200°C

SATURN
-288°F
-178°C

JUPITER
-234°F
-145°C

ROCKY PLANETS AND GAS GIANTS

The four planets closest to the sun are made of rocks and metals, with rocky surfaces that a spacecraft could land on. Past the Asteroid Belt are the giant planets. These are made of gas — their surfaces are not solid at all. They are many times bigger, far colder, and much farther apart than the rocky planets. You can see the relative distances between the planets in the diagram below.

Mercury
Earth
Mars
Jupiter
Saturn
Uranus
Neptune
Venus

This chart shows how far the planets are from the sun and each other!

EARTH VS. MARS

Who would win in a contest between Earth and Mars?

Despite sitting beside one another in the solar system, the two planets are very different. Mars is farther from the sun, making it much colder — its average temperature is a freezing -81°F (-63°C).

A day on Mars is just half an hour longer than a day on Earth. However, Mars moves around the sun at a slower speed than Earth, which means a year lasts much longer. One year on Mars is 687 Earth days — a long wait between birthdays!

You can see Earth and Mars from space, but Mars is smaller in size — six of it could fit inside one Earth! Gravity on Mars is much weaker, too. You would weigh about one-third of your Earth weight there, so you could jump much higher.

EARTH

MARS

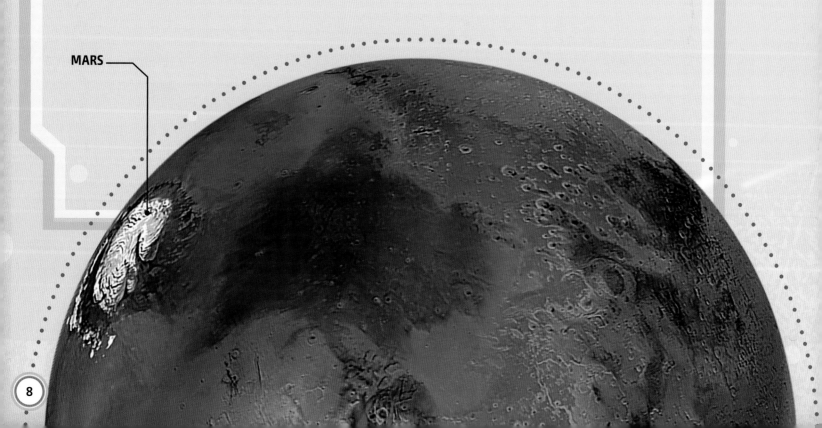

THE FACTS

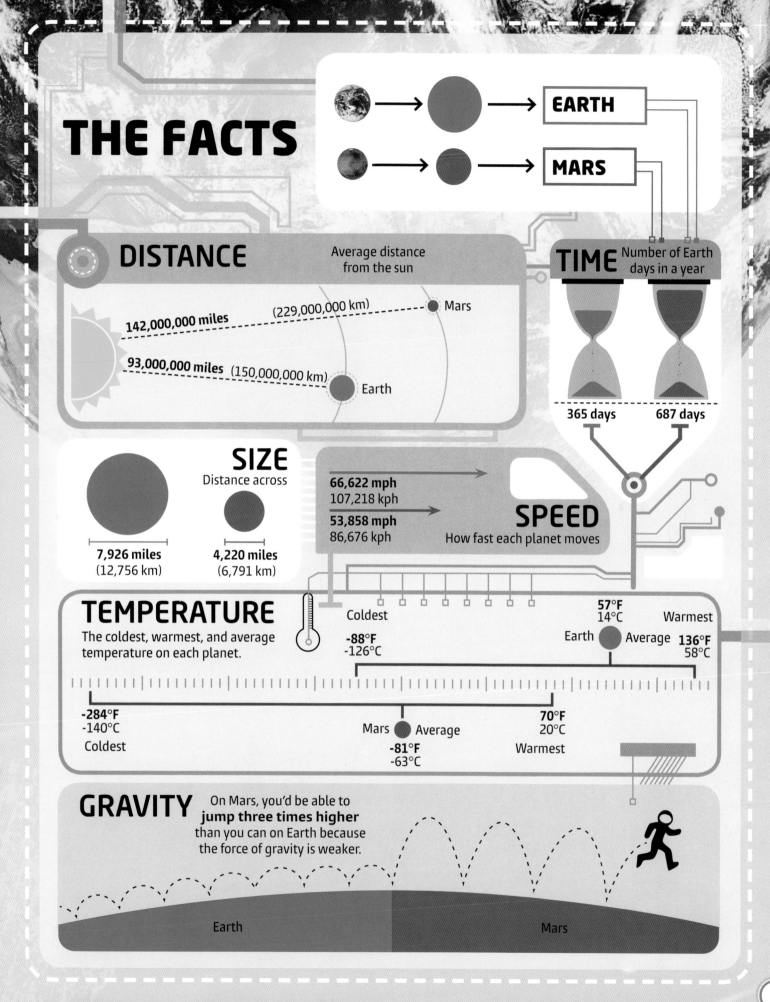

EARTH

MARS

DISTANCE
Average distance from the sun

142,000,000 miles (229,000,000 km) ········ Mars

93,000,000 miles (150,000,000 km) ········ Earth

TIME
Number of Earth days in a year

365 days   687 days

SIZE
Distance across

7,926 miles (12,756 km)

4,220 miles (6,791 km)

66,622 mph
107,218 kph

53,858 mph
86,676 kph

SPEED
How fast each planet moves

TEMPERATURE
The coldest, warmest, and average temperature on each planet.

Coldest

-88°F
-126°C

57°F
14°C   Warmest

Earth ● Average   136°F
58°C

-284°F
-140°C

Coldest

Mars ● Average

-81°F
-63°C

70°F
20°C

Warmest

GRAVITY
On Mars, you'd be able to **jump three times higher** than you can on Earth because the force of gravity is weaker.

Earth   Mars

A ROCKY RED PLANET

Mars is made of rock, like the Earth. Its surface is a rusty red color and the planet glows red in the night sky.

Mars has mountains and valleys, like Earth, but they are much bigger. On Earth, flowing water and strong winds have worn the surface down. Mars does not have flowing water and its wind is much weaker than Earth's, so the moutains are taller and the valleys deeper. However, scientists do think that Mars and Earth formed in similar ways.

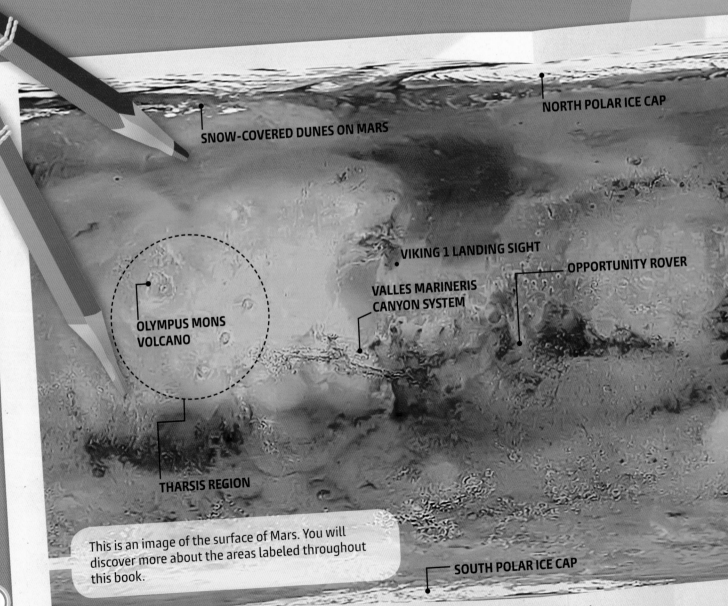

NORTH POLAR ICE CAP

SNOW-COVERED DUNES ON MARS

VIKING 1 LANDING SIGHT

OPPORTUNITY ROVER

VALLES MARINERIS CANYON SYSTEM

OLYMPUS MONS VOLCANO

THARSIS REGION

This is an image of the surface of Mars. You will discover more about the areas labeled throughout this book.

SOUTH POLAR ICE CAP

A robot has wiped away dust to reveal the red surface of Mars.

WHAT IS ON THE SURFACE?

The surface of Mars is dusty and dry. Spacecraft investigating it have taken pictures of tall volcanoes, deep craters, and valleys that look like they once contained rivers. The northern half of Mars is mostly smooth, flat ground with a few huge volcanoes. The southern half is very different, with large, high-up areas and bumpy craters.

A hole dug in the surface of Mars by a rover shows the rusty red color of the soil underneath.

Rocks on the surface of Mars

WHY IS IT RED?

The rocks on the surface of Mars contain a lot of iron, a metal that also appears on Earth. When iron reacts with oxygen in the air, it rusts and turns reddish-orange, like an old bike when it is left outside. It is the rusty rocks that make Mars look red. Some places on Earth have iron-rich soil that is a similar color, such as Hawaii and Australia.

INSIGHT LANDING SITE

CURIOSITY ROVER

SPIRIT ROVER

GALE CRATER

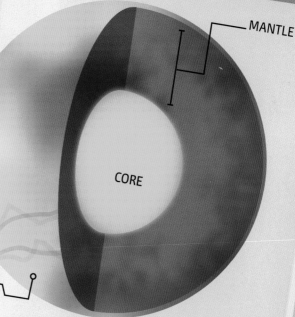

MANTLE

CORE

CRUST

WHAT IS INSIDE MARS?

Mars has three layers, like Earth. There is a rocky crust on the outside, a soft area under the crust called the mantle, and a core at the center. We don't yet know how big these layers are, or if the core is solid or liquid. A NASA spacecraft named InSight landed on Mars in 2018. Its job is to measure vibrations in the ground to discover more about these layers.

THE CLIMATE ON MARS

Today, Mars is a cold, dry desert with no liquid water on its surface. Some scientists, however, think that it might once have been warm and wet.

Rocky valleys and large bowl-shaped dips on the planet show that Mars once had rivers, lakes, and seas. For ice to melt and allow these rivers to flow, Mars would have had to be much warmer. The temperature of a planet is affected by how far away from the sun it is, but also by its atmosphere — the air around it. Many scientists believe a change in Mars's atmosphere has made it much colder than it used to be.

BEFORE

WHAT WAS MARS LIKE IN THE PAST?

About 4 billion years ago, Mars had a thicker atmosphere that could hold more heat. We don't know exactly what the temperature was, but it was probably warmer than today. This would mean water was liquid, not frozen, and so the planet was also wetter.

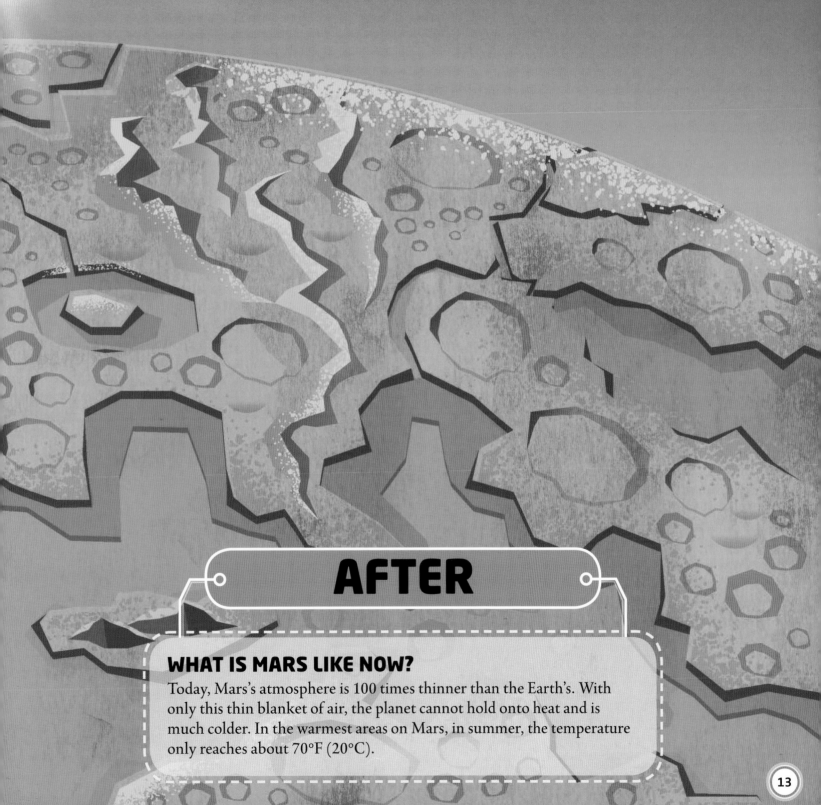

WHAT IS ATMOSPHERE?

An atmosphere is the air that wraps around a planet. It is made up of a mixture of gases — each planet's mixture is different. An atmosphere acts like a greenhouse, absorbing some of the sun's heat and keeping the planet warm. Mars has a very thin atmosphere now, so it is cold. Earth's atmosphere is thick, which is why it is warm here. The mixture of gases in our atmosphere allows plants and animals to live and breathe.

AFTER

WHAT IS MARS LIKE NOW?

Today, Mars's atmosphere is 100 times thinner than the Earth's. With only this thin blanket of air, the planet cannot hold onto heat and is much colder. In the warmest areas on Mars, in summer, the temperature only reaches about 70°F (20°C).

01.

THE PAST:

"WHAT HAS HAPPENED ON MARS SO FAR?"

People believe all sorts of things about Mars's past, but not all of them are true. This image shows some of the things you will discover in this chapter, from the made-up idea of aliens on Mars to the fact that it is named after the Roman god of war. Read on to discover what might actually have happened in Mars's past.

MARS IN HISTORY

Imagine you didn't know about stars or planets. If you looked up and saw bright lights in the night sky, what would you think they were?

We now know these are mostly stars and planets, but people in the past haven't always known this. They saw lights in the sky and would tell stories about what they thought they were. They noticed the lights moved through the sky throughout the day and night, and some were much brighter than others. One light was particularly intriguing, with a striking red color and a path that moved backward and forward across the sky. We now know this is Mars!

NAMING THE RED PLANET

Many people in ancient times believed that the planets were linked to their gods in some way, and they connected the mysterious planet to their gods of war. In ancient Greece, the god of war was named Ares. Later, in ancient Rome, he was called Mars — this name for the Red Planet stuck!

A statue of Mars, the Roman god of war

Mars

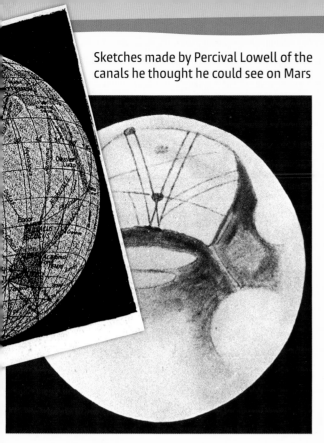

Sketches made by Percival Lowell of the canals he thought he could see on Mars

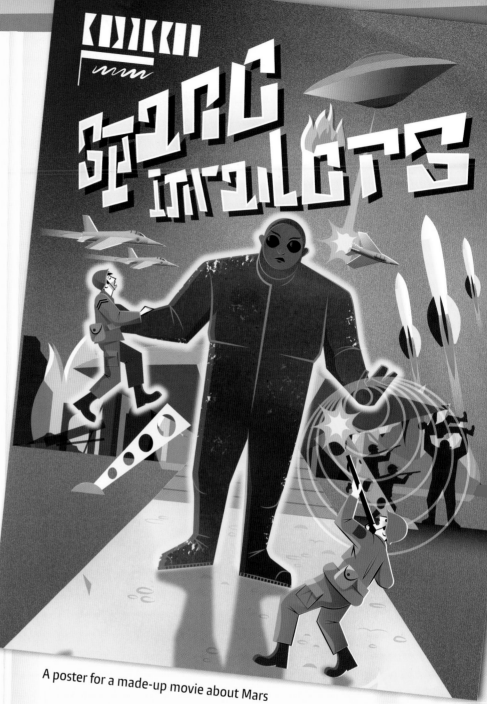

A poster for a made-up movie about Mars

CURIOUS CANALS

Over time, people realized that the planets were worlds orbiting the sun, like Earth. As telescopes (invented in the early 1600s) improved, scientists turned them to the planets and looked for features on their surfaces.

In the 1800s, astronomers reported seeing straight lines on the surface of Mars. Astronomer Percival Lowell decided that they formed a network of canals made by intelligent beings. We now know that there aren't any water-filled canals on the surface of Mars. The lines seen by astronomers may have been the valleys that we now know cover Mars's surface.

MARTIAN FICTION

As people learned about Mars, they started to realize that it could have been home to a form of life. In about 1895, around the same time that Percival Lowell was studying Mars, British author H. G. Wells wrote *The War of the Worlds* — a story about martians coming from their dying planet to invade Earth. Ever since, people have been fascinated by the idea of martian invaders visiting Earth, or travelers to Mars finding strange aliens living there.

THE YOUNG SUN

HOW DID MARS FORM?

The planets, including Mars, formed from leftover material when the sun was born.

The solar system began as a huge gas and dust cloud, which was slowly pulled together by a force called gravity. When enough material had collected in one place, the core heated up to create a new star, our sun. More material clumped around the sun to form lumps of rock and chunks of ice, liquid, and gas. Some of these blobs clumped to form even bigger ones — planets. Scientists don't yet understand exactly how this happened, and they are still finding clues to try to explain what took place.

1 SMALL COLLISIONS

As the solar system was forming, thousands of rock clusters swirled around the young sun. These crashed into each another, sometimes breaking into pieces, but other times sticking together. Over time, a few clumps got bigger by collecting up the smaller rocks around them.

2

A BALL FORMS

Some big blobs began to form into balls. This is because gravity pulled on them from their center to their edges, creating a round shape. One of these objects was the young Mars. The heavier materials in the ball, such as metals, sank to the center and formed a core. This movement inside the planet created a huge amount of heat, which melted rocks and may have formed a sea of liquid rock on Mars's surface.

CAN YOU IMAGINE?

The processes on this page didn't happen quickly. In fact, they took place over such a long time that humans would struggle to put it into words. They also happened at temperatures so hot and so cold that they are very hard to imagine!

3

MARS COOLS DOWN

Eventually, the planet cooled and the lava hardened into a crust. At the same time, leftover pieces of rock crashed into the planet, leaving big craters on its new surface. Heat deep inside the planet caused volcanoes and lava flows to appear and change the shape of the crust. Eventually, Mars cooled so much that the volcanoes stopped erupting.

CRATERS ON MARS

When a rock crashes into a planet, it leaves a round hole called a crater. All the rocky planets, including Mars and Earth, have craters on their surfaces.

If a space rock makes it through the atmosphere and hits the surface of the planet, we call it a meteorite. A large meteorite can make a crater that is 10 times its size. When the solar system was new, millions of meteorites crashed into the rocky planets, making craters. Most of the craters on Earth have been smoothed away or filled in by rain, volcanoes, and plant and animal life. However, these things don't exist on Mars, so we can still see lots of its craters. Looking at Mars helps us learn the story of what has happened to Earth.

COUNTING CRATERS

Craters can tell us more than just where meteorites have hit a planet. By counting craters, we can figure out the age of an area of a planet's surface. The more craters there are, the older the area is.

HOW DO CRATERS FORM?

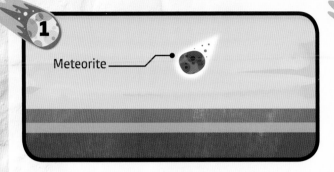

1

Meteorite

A meteorite falls toward a planet, heating up as it moves through the atmosphere. Small rocks burn up, but large ones smash into the ground.

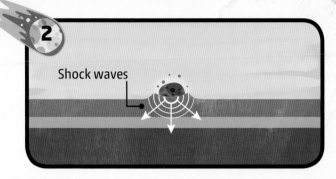

2

Shock waves

The meteorite is traveling very fast when it smashes into the surface. The force of this sends vibrations, called shock waves, into the ground.

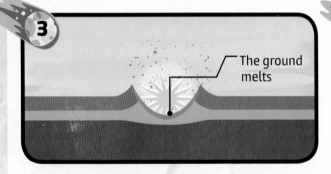

3

The ground melts

The crash quickly heats up the meteorite, which explodes, throwing out rock and gas. The explosion melts the ground and causes some rock to turn into gas, leaving a crater.

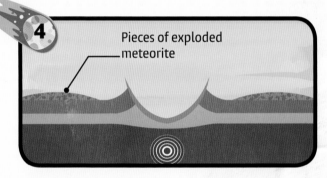

4

Pieces of exploded meteorite

The ground below the crash, which got pushed down by the shock waves, pushes back up. The pieces of exploded meteorite fall on the ground around the crater.

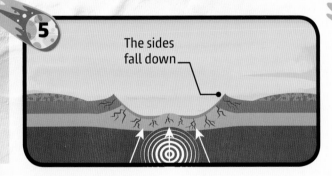

5

The sides fall down

As the ground pushes up, the sides of the crater crack and fall down. The ground sometimes pushes up enough to make a hill in the middle of the crater.

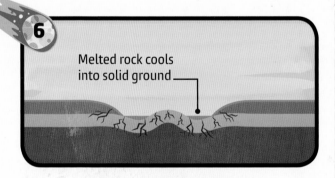

6

Melted rock cools into solid ground

The hot melted rock cools and becomes solid. The round crater shows where the meteorite hit. This crater may remain unchanged for thousands of years.

MARTIAN MOONS

Imagine looking into the night sky and seeing not one moon, but two!

Mars's moons are called Phobos and Deimos. They are not round, like Earth's moon, but lumpy, like potatoes. Scientists are thinking about using the moons as a base. From here, they could study the moons in more detail, or they could use the base as a handy stop-off on the way to Mars. The moons are named after the sons of Mars, the Roman god of war. Phobos means "fear" or "panic," and Deimos means "dread," or "fleeing from battle." They were discovered and named in 1877 by US astronomer Asaph Hall.

PHOBOS

Phobos orbits Mars quickly and closely. It is gradually spiraling closer to Mars, getting about 6 ft (1.8 m) closer to the surface every hundred years. Within 50 million years, scientists predict that Phobos will either break up and form a ring around Mars, or will crash into it in a collision strong enough to kill anything on the planet.

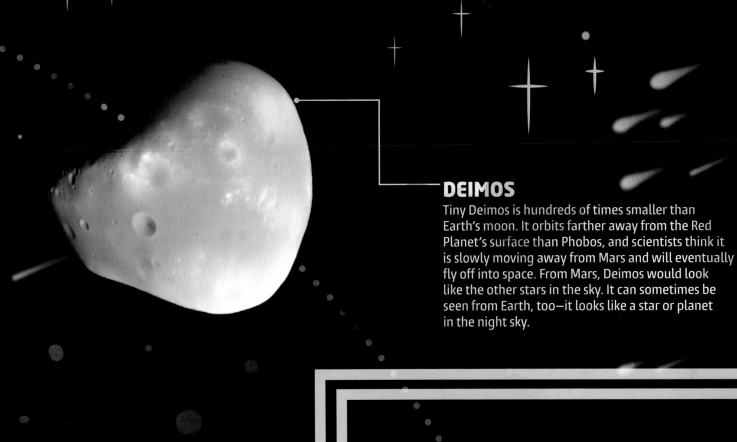

DEIMOS

Tiny Deimos is hundreds of times smaller than Earth's moon. It orbits farther away from the Red Planet's surface than Phobos, and scientists think it is slowly moving away from Mars and will eventually fly off into space. From Mars, Deimos would look like the other stars in the sky. It can sometimes be seen from Earth, too—it looks like a star or planet in the night sky.

TINY MOONS OR ASTEROIDS?

Mars's moons are very small — Phobos is 157 times smaller than Earth's moon, and Deimos is 280 times smaller. Scientists don't know a lot about the moons, but think they could be asteroids that were pulled in by the gravity of Mars, or lumps of rock left over from when Mars was formed way back in the past.

SIZE
Distance across each moon

DEIMOS
7.8 miles
12.6 km

PHOBOS
13.8 miles
22.2 km

EARTH'S MOON
2,158.8 miles
3,474.2 km

VOLCANIC ERUPTIONS

Mars is home to the biggest volcanoes in the solar system, many of which are far larger than any mountain on Earth.

The biggest of all is Olympus Mons (see pages 40–41), but there are several other giant volcanoes — plus many smaller ones — that formed in different ways. We've never seen an eruption on Mars, so it seems that most volcanoes are now extinct (or have at least been asleep for millions of years).

THE THARSIS VOLCANOES

A huge volcanic region, known as the Tharsis region, is home to 12 large volcanoes. Four of these (including Olympus Mons) are the biggest on Mars. They sit around a huge bulge on Mars's surface called the Tharsis Rise. Scientists think that Tharsis is on top of a "hot spot" — a fountain of hot material from deep inside Mars. This hot spot kept the rocks just under the surface molten and supplied the volcanoes with molten lava for billions of years.

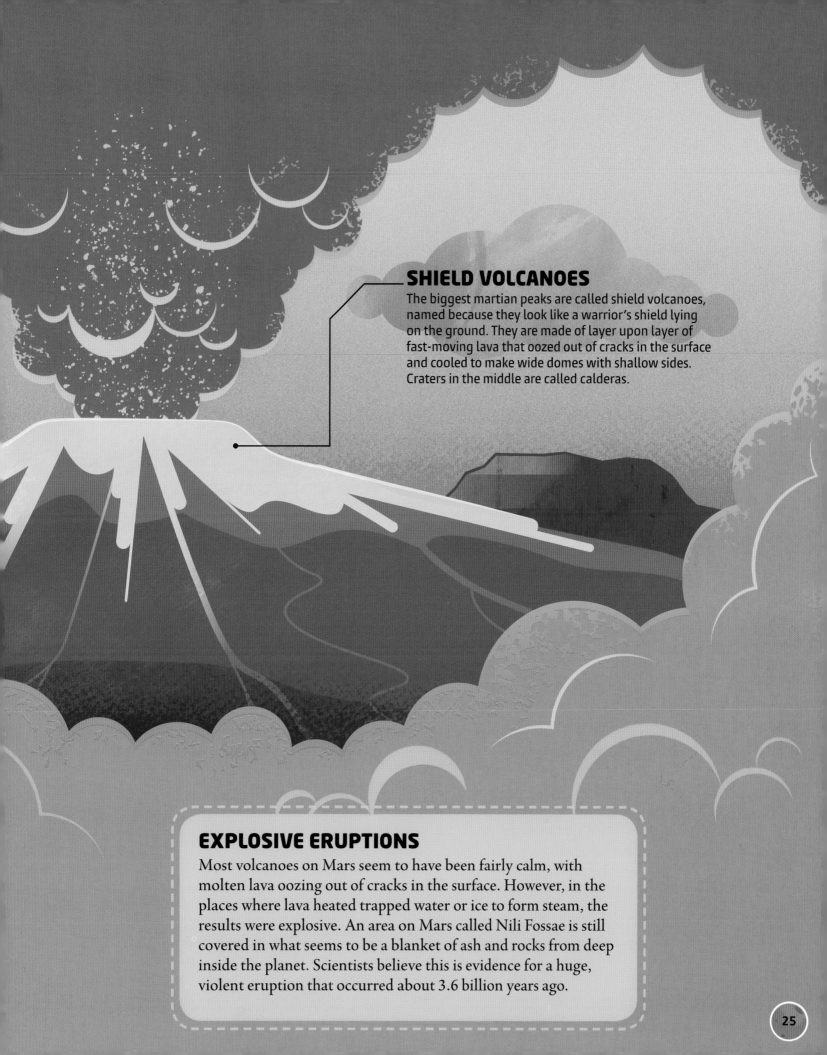

SHIELD VOLCANOES

The biggest martian peaks are called shield volcanoes, named because they look like a warrior's shield lying on the ground. They are made of layer upon layer of fast-moving lava that oozed out of cracks in the surface and cooled to make wide domes with shallow sides. Craters in the middle are called calderas.

EXPLOSIVE ERUPTIONS

Most volcanoes on Mars seem to have been fairly calm, with molten lava oozing out of cracks in the surface. However, in the places where lava heated trapped water or ice to form steam, the results were explosive. An area on Mars called Nili Fossae is still covered in what seems to be a blanket of ash and rocks from deep inside the planet. Scientists believe this is evidence for a huge, violent eruption that occurred about 3.6 billion years ago.

WATER ON MARS

Scientists know that there was liquid water on Mars and that it shaped a lot of the planet's surface. But they still don't know how much water was there or how long it was there.

Mars was once warm enough to have rivers and lakes, like Earth. There is still some water on Mars today, but it is not easy to see or find — it is frozen as ice or hidden in rocks underground. Now, Mars looks dry and desertlike, but its rocks tell the story of how water once flowed like it does on Earth. The shapes and patterns of the rocks, as well as what is inside them, can be used to figure out where water might have been and what it was like.

RIVERS—JUST LIKE EARTH!

Scientists have spotted clues that there were once rivers on Mars. Patterns in the ground, which look like the branches of a tree, are similar to patterns made by rivers on Earth. This makes scientists think that there were rivers on Mars, too. Robots have discovered smooth rocks on Mars. Rocks on Earth become smooth and round after being tumbled along the ground by rivers. Scientists believe the same thing may have happened to the smooth rocks on Mars.

OCEANS AND LAKES ON MARS

Earth is covered with oceans and lakes where water has filled in large, deep dips in the ground. On Mars, there might have been one big ocean in the northern half of the planet. Curiosity Rover, a robot sent to Mars in 2011 to gather information about past living things and water on Mars (pages 46–47), landed in a dip (known as Gale Crater) that scientists think used to be a lake. It tested the rocks and found that the water was probably salty and acidic — not like water on Earth. Scientists believe, however, that there could still have been living things there.

This image shows what Mars might have looked like when it had water on its surface in the past.

DOES WATER MEAN LIFE?

There may never have been life on the Red Planet, but the fact that there was water on Mars makes scientists think that life might have existed there. Living things on Earth need water to survive, so we have used water as our guide when looking for life on Mars. However, it's also possible that something has lived on Mars that does not need water to survive—an exciting idea that we don't understand yet!

This is an artist's idea of what Gale Crater, which is now dry, might have looked like if it had been filled with water.

LIFE ON MARS?

One of the most exciting questions scientists are trying to answer is if there ever was, or still is, life on Mars.

Based on what we know from Earth, life needs a few things to exist—carbon (a chemical element that helps to form other chemicals essential for life), liquid water, and a source of energy such as sunlight. Evidence from orbiters and robotic rovers shows that Mars had all of these things in the distant past. So did life ever appear there? And if it did, could it still survive today?

MARS

This photograph shows our galaxy, the Milky Way, from Earth.

DID LIFE COME FROM MARS?

Conditions on Mars and Earth have changed a lot over time. Mars's conditions may have been suitable for life hundreds of millions of years before Earth's conditions were suitable. So could life on Earth actually have started on Mars? Several meteorites (rocks from space found on Earth) have turned out to be chunks of Mars, blasted away from the planet a long time ago. Some people have suggested that they could have carried microscopic living things from Mars to Earth. Although it's an exciting idea, so far there is no real evidence to back it up.

THE MEANING OF LIFE

Mars is the nearest planet to Earth with conditions that were once suitable for life. It is the only planet, other than Earth, that we've investigated in any detail so far. If we found that living things did once exist on Mars, it would open up the amazing possibility that life could exist where conditions are right. Such places could be somewhere in the wider universe or even on the outer planets in our own solar system.

02.

THE PRESENT:

"WHAT ARE WE LEARNING ABOUT MARS NOW?"

This picture shows the launch of Curiosity Rover, a spacecraft sent to Mars in
2011 to discover more about the planet. Find out more on pages 46-47

WHAT'S IT LIKE ON MARS?

Like any place you've never visited before, you can only imagine what it might be like on Mars.

No human has been to the Red Planet yet, but robots have taken pictures and measurements that tell us a lot about the conditions there. Anyone visiting Mars would have to be inside a space suit or shelter the whole time to protect them from the dangerous conditions on the planet. But let's imagine that you are on Mars and can step outside without protection, like you do on Earth. What do your senses tell you about the Red Planet?

MARTIAN SUNSET

This is an artist's idea of how the sunset would look if you were standing on Mars. The sky turns from pink to blue as the sun sets.

WHAT CAN YOU SENSE?

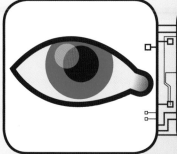

WHAT CAN YOU SEE?

During the day, the sky is a pinkish-orange color, and as the sun sets it becomes blue. The sun looks smaller than it does from Earth. Mars's dusty, orange ground is scattered with boulders, and you might be able to see hills, sand dunes, or huge mountains in the distance.

WHAT CAN YOU SMELL?

Hold your nose! A disgusting smell of rotten eggs is coming from the soil — a chemical called sulfur makes it smell like this. There's also carbon dioxide in the atmosphere, which burns your nose with its sharp, acidic smell.

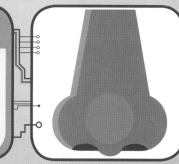

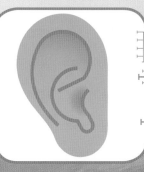

WHAT CAN YOU HEAR?

As you walk over the ground, the soil beneath your feet squishes softly. You can hear the clank of a spacecraft's robotic arm moving nearby. It is probably quieter than you are used to because sound waves can't travel as well through the thin atmopshere.

WHAT CAN YOU FEEL?

Mars has less gravity than Earth, so you feel much lighter and can bounce three times higher. The thin atmosphere (pages 12–13) means that heat escapes from the ground so quickly that the temperature at your feet feels warmer than up by your head!

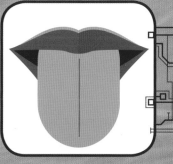

WHAT CAN YOU TASTE?

After a sandstorm, the iron-rich dust in the air tastes like metal. You don't want to breathe too deeply — each breath of atmosphere you take turns to acid in your mouth and tastes horrible!

HOW WE EXPLORE

We send different types of spacecraft to Mars to gather information that we can't get from Earth.

Scientists must choose which type of spacecraft is best for each mission to Mars. Every mission builds on the last one, like steps going up a staircase. First, scientists send flying spacecraft to take pictures and find a place to land. Then, spacecraft land on the surface. Information from these missions is used to design rovers to drive around on the planet to learn even more. Here are some different types of spacecraft. Which one would you send to Mars next?

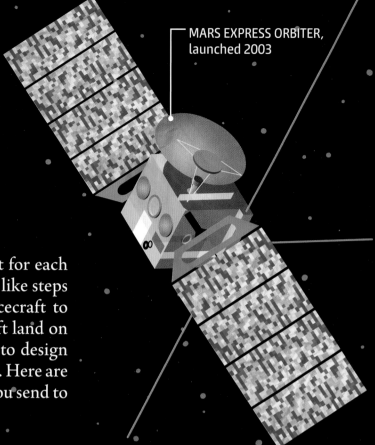

MARS EXPRESS ORBITER, launched 2003

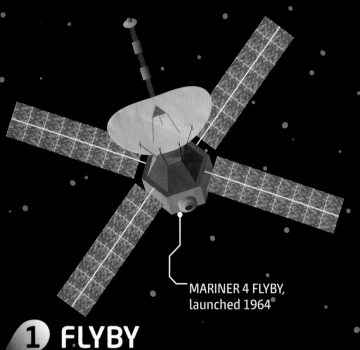

MARINER 4 FLYBY, launched 1964

1 FLYBY

The simplest kind of mission is a flyby. The spacecraft flies past a planet once, so is a good way to find out basic information. A flyby can be completed quickly because it does not have to slow down to orbit the planet. The first mission to Mars was the Mariner 4 flyby, launched in 1964. It took pictures of Mars's surface and atmosphere.

2 ORBITER

To get closer to a planet than a flyby, scientists send an orbiter. This kind of spacecraft circles around a planet or moon for months or years. It takes lots of pictures, like weather satellites do for the Earth. Orbiters can also pass messages and information from spacecraft on a planet's surface back to Earth. One orbiter that has been studying the Red Planet since 2003 is the Mars Express.

③ LANDER

Once spacecraft from orbit have collected information about a planet, a lander can be sent to touch down on its surface. Landers stay in one place and test the soil, rocks, and weather conditions at their site. Landing on a planet is much harder than orbiting, so this kind of mission is risky. The most successful lander misison to another planet was the Viking 1, which landed on Mars in 1976. It discovered new things about Mars's atmosphere and its rocks and soil.

④ ROVER

The most complicated type of mission is a rover — a spacecraft with wheels that is released onto a planet (sometimes by a lander) where it drives around like a car. A rover requires careful design so it can drive over rough ground on a planet without getting stuck. Rovers can get close-up measurements of the planet's features and can climb hills to see more. The longest mission of this type was the Opportunity rover, which launched in 2003 and spent more than 14 years studying Mars.

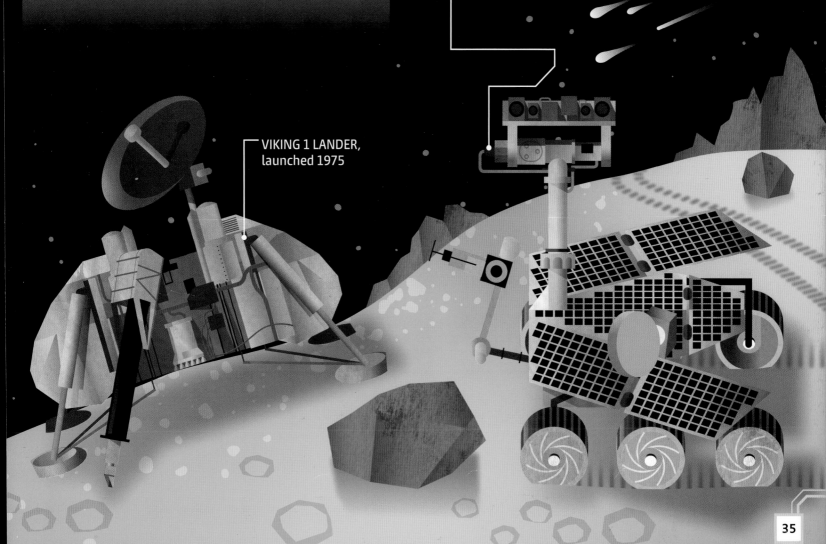

OPPORTUNITY ROVER,
launched 2003

VIKING 1 LANDER,
launched 1975

1 ENTRY

The lander, contained in a shell, hits Mars's atmosphere. Hot gases turn the outside of the shell as hot as the surface of the sun. However, the lander inside barely reaches room temperature, thanks to its protective shell.

2 PARACHUTE

Once the atmosphere has slowed the shell down to about 1,000 mph (1,600 kph), special parachutes designed for high speeds are released to slow it down even more. It is now 6 miles (10 km) from Mars's surface.

3 CABLE

Just 35 seconds later, when it has slowed to about 200 mph (320 kph), the lander pops out of the shell. It hangs 65 ft (20 m) below the shell on a thin (not much thicker than a shoelace), but very strong cable.

LANDING ON MARS IS HARD!

A lander approaching Mars is traveling at speeds of thousands of miles per hour and must slow down to zero before reaching it.

If the lander doesn't slow down enough, it might smash into the planet, destroying itself and ending the whole mission. This incredible deceleration has to happen in as little as six minutes — the time it takes for the lander to travel from Mars's atmosphere to its surface.

Engineers have found ways to slow down the lander very quickly to stop it from crash-landing — here is one of them. The lander does this on its own, making decisions itself, since signals take too long to travel from Mars to Earth for humans to be able to control it.

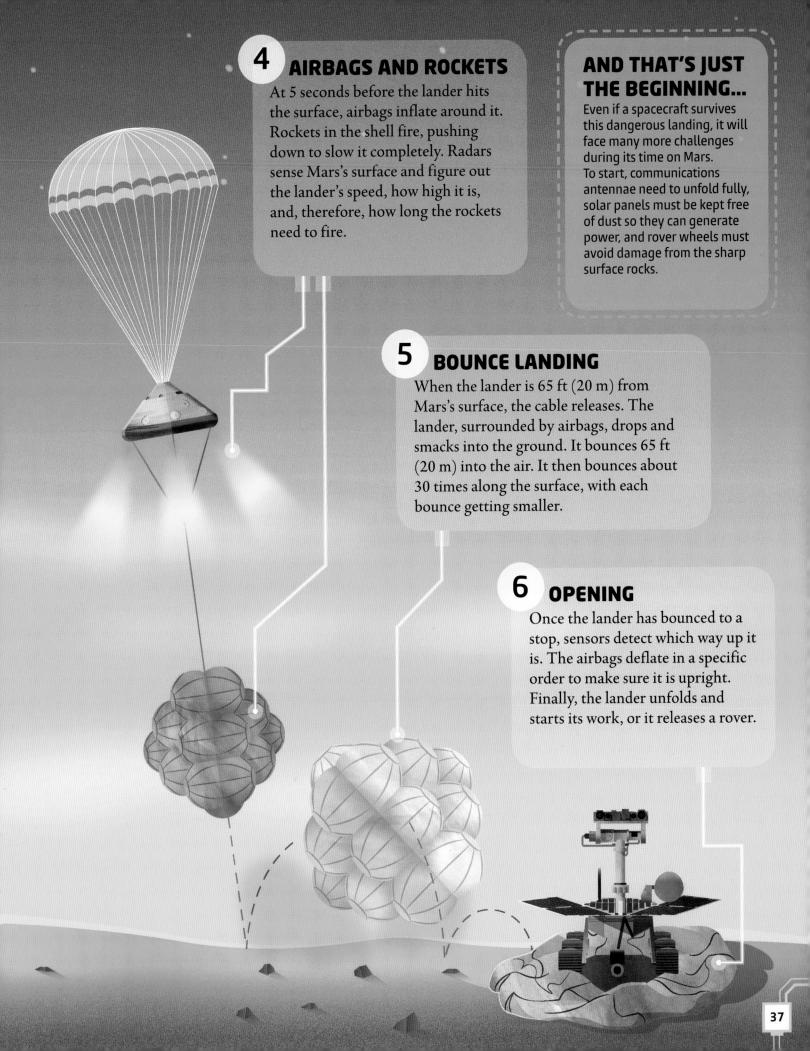

4 AIRBAGS AND ROCKETS

At 5 seconds before the lander hits the surface, airbags inflate around it. Rockets in the shell fire, pushing down to slow it completely. Radars sense Mars's surface and figure out the lander's speed, how high it is, and, therefore, how long the rockets need to fire.

AND THAT'S JUST THE BEGINNING...

Even if a spacecraft survives this dangerous landing, it will face many more challenges during its time on Mars. To start, communications antennae need to unfold fully, solar panels must be kept free of dust so they can generate power, and rover wheels must avoid damage from the sharp surface rocks.

5 BOUNCE LANDING

When the lander is 65 ft (20 m) from Mars's surface, the cable releases. The lander, surrounded by airbags, drops and smacks into the ground. It bounces 65 ft (20 m) into the air. It then bounces about 30 times along the surface, with each bounce getting smaller.

6 OPENING

Once the lander has bounced to a stop, sensors detect which way up it is. The airbags deflate in a specific order to make sure it is upright. Finally, the lander unfolds and starts its work, or it releases a rover.

VALLES MARINERIS

You cannot miss Valles Marineris — a huge crack in Mars's crust as long as the United States! See how it compares to one of the biggest, most famous valleys on Earth — the Grand Canyon.

LOCATION

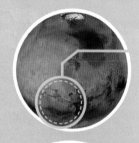

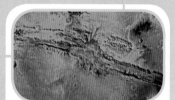

VALLES MARINERIS, MARS

GRAND CANYON, USA

LENGTH

How far each valley stretches

**GRAND CANYON
500 miles
(800 km)**

**VALLES MARINERIS
2,500 miles
(4,000 km)**

DEPTH

Distance from the bottom to the top

**GRAND CANYON
1 mile
(1.6 km)**

**VALLES MARINERIS
5 miles
(8 km)**

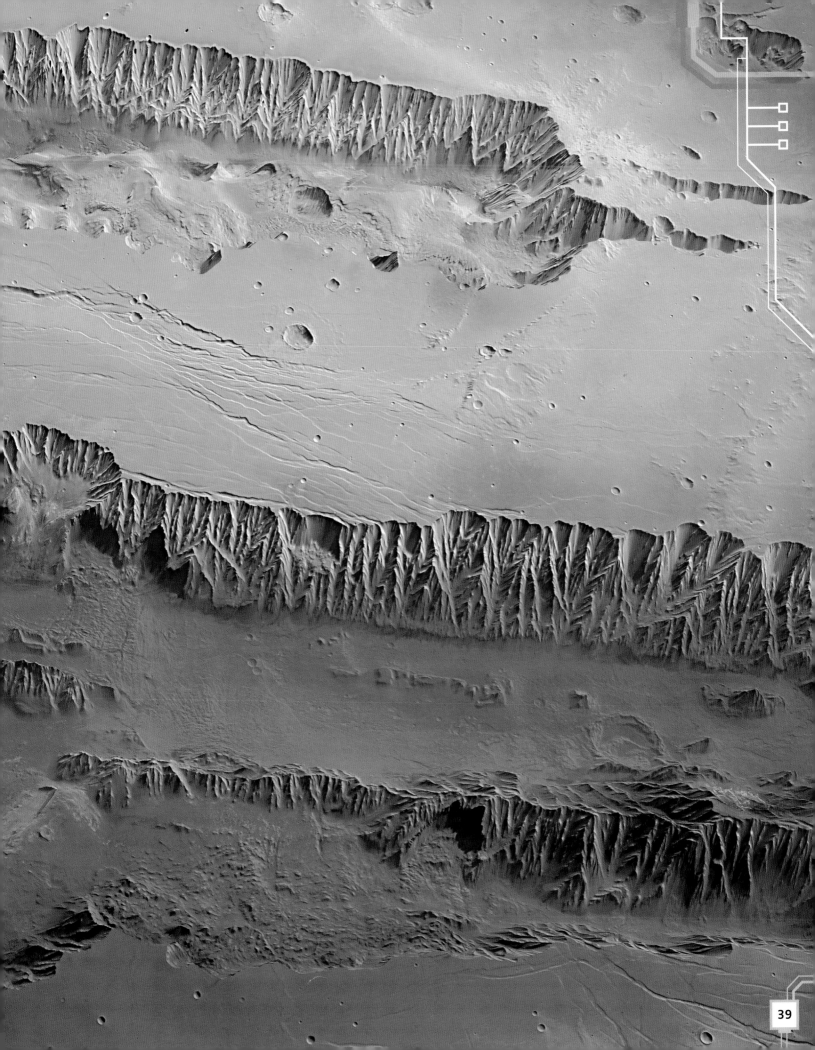

OLYMPUS MONS

The biggest volcano in the solar system, Olympus Mons lies a little north of Mars's equator. It is a type of volcano known as a shield volcano (see pages 24–25). Formed by lava erupting for about two billion years, the volcano rises high above the flat ground that surrounds it. There are overlapping craters in its center that plunge 2 miles (3.2 km) deep. Olympus Mons is incredibly wide — about the width of the state of Arizona. It has gentle slopes, but they end in cliffs around its edge. These cliffs soar up to 5 miles (8 km) high.

FACT FILE

Everything about Olympus Mons is on a massive scale. It even dwarfs Mount Everest — the highest mountain on Earth.

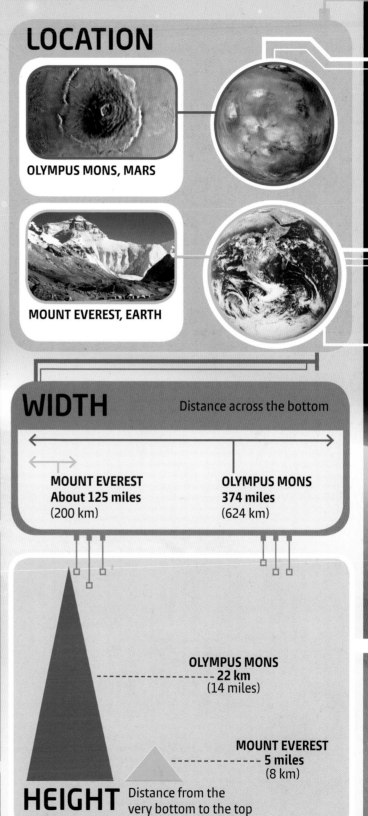

LOCATION

OLYMPUS MONS, MARS

MOUNT EVEREST, EARTH

WIDTH
Distance across the bottom

MOUNT EVEREST
About 125 miles
(200 km)

OLYMPUS MONS
374 miles
(624 km)

OLYMPUS MONS
22 km
(14 miles)

MOUNT EVEREST
5 miles
(8 km)

HEIGHT
Distance from the very bottom to the top

MEASURING MARS

In 2018, a lander named InSight arrived on Mars, ready to give the planet its first checkup since it formed 4.5 billion years ago.

Unlike the Curiosity rover, which can drive around, the InSight lander has no wheels and stays in one place. Scientists use InSight to understand what is inside Mars. By studying the temperature deep underground and measuring "Marsquakes," InSight helps us figure out what the ground under the surface is like, and if it is like the soil on Earth. Answering these questions will also help us discover if the stories of how Earth and Mars were formed are the same. If they aren't the same, scientists want to find out why. InSight has a few instruments to help it study Mars: a robotic arm for performing tasks; a seismometer (an instrument that measures the movement of the ground); and the "mole" (an instrument that measures temperature).

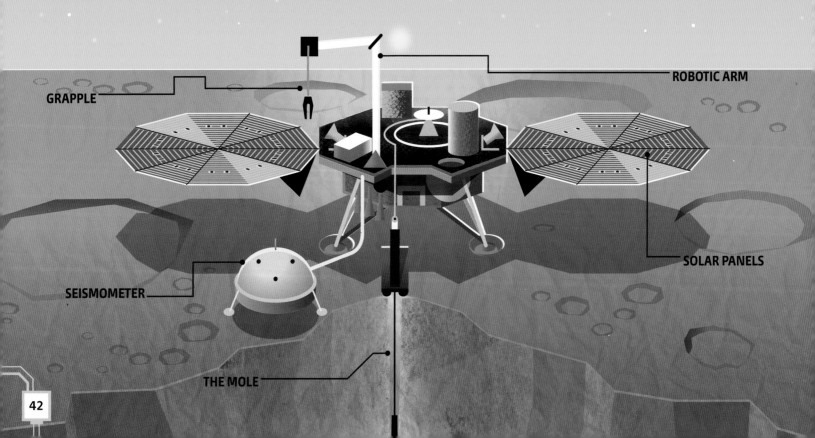

GRAPPLE

ROBOTIC ARM

SOLAR PANELS

SEISMOMETER

THE MOLE

WHAT DOES INSIGHT DO?

MARSQUAKES

Both Earth and Mars have layers of rock inside them, but we cannot dig deep enough to see them. To learn about the rock inside Earth, scientists study how earthquakes move through the ground. InSight's seismometer studies the same thing on Mars. Like a doctor's stethoscope listening for heartbeats, it listens for "Marsquakes."

The image above shows InSight's seismometer. It is covered by a dome-shaped shield, which protects it from the extreme temperatures on Mars. In addition to quakes in the ground, it can also sense the vibrations created by winds and storms.

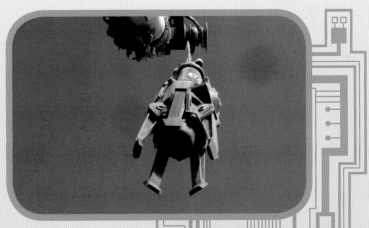

GOING DEEPER!

InSight is the first robot that can dig more than an inch or so below the surface of Mars. It has an instrument known as the "mole," which pokes into the ground like a nail into wood. On the end is a thermometer to take the temperature under the ground. Unfortunately, the mole hasn't managed to dig very deep into the ground so far.

The image above shows InSight's grapple, which is a grabbing tool attached to its robotic arm. The grapple's five mechanical fingers work like a hand to close around objects and grip them. This allows the arm to lift things and assist with tricky tasks.

The image on the right is a selfie taken by InSight. You can see a thin coating of red dust covering the spacecraft.

SAND DETECTIVES

Scientists can study the wind on Mars without ever visiting the planet by looking for clues like a detective. They look at the sand dunes—hills of sand that get moved by the wind. The shape of the dunes shows which direction the wind is blowing and how it has changed. The picture on this page was taken by a spacecraft looking down at sand dunes on Mars. The sand is actually gray, although the spacecraft camera makes it look blue.

WIND AND WEATHER

Mars has wind, weather, and seasons that change throughout the year. Seasons are caused by a planet being tilted — the part of the planet that is tilted toward the sun warms up to cause summer weather, and the area tilted away gets winter weather. Mars has a tilt similar to Earth's, and it also has four seasons. Snow and frost appear during winter, while dust storms can cover huge areas in the summer. Even in summer, though, Mars is much colder than Earth.

The atmosphere on Mars is so thin that wind cannot push very hard. Winds on Mars can be as fast as the speed of a car driving on the highway, but they are less powerful than on Earth. To fly a kite on Mars, the wind would need to blow much faster than it would on Earth to get the kite into the air.

DUST STORMS

Dust storms form when the winds on Mars blow clouds of dust into the air. These storms can stay in one small area or cover the entire planet. Mars also gets dust devils, like the one shown here. These are incredible spinning towers of sand that can be as tall as a mountain.

CURIOSITY ROVER

One of the most interesting spacecraft to be sent to Mars is Curiosity, a rock-blasting rover.

In 2012, NASA's Curiosity rover landed in Gale Crater on Mars. The rover is the size of a small car and is controlled by scientists on Earth. Its job is to find out as much as it can about the planet. Seventeen cameras take photos to learn more about Mars. They include ChemCam, which fires a laser to identify chemicals in rocks and soil. Curiosity searches for water, collects data on Mars's climate, and looks for signs of past or present life in the ground. Investigating Mars is slow work, though — the rover travels only 1½ in (3.8 cm) each second and has traveled a mere 12.5 miles (20 km) since landing on Mars.

CURIOSITY: MARS ROVER

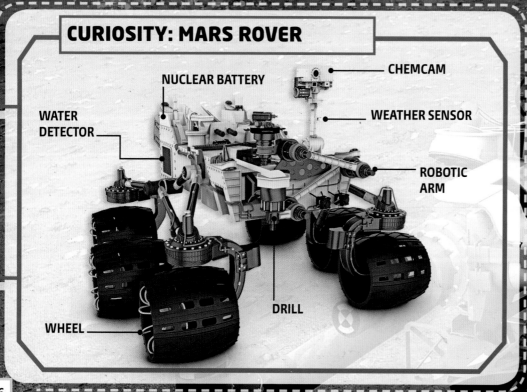

WATER DETECTOR

NUCLEAR BATTERY

CHEMCAM

WEATHER SENSOR

ROBOTIC ARM

DRILL

WHEEL

LASER POWER

Curiosity's smartest tool is called ChemCam. It combines a superpowered invisible laser, a small telescope, and a camera to learn about rocks on Mars. The laser fires blasts of heat at targets up to 23 ft (7 m) away, turning them into hot gas. The camera photographs the melting rock through the telescope and measures the colors of the gas being given off, which tells scientists what the rock is made of. ChemCam can record more than 6,000 different colors (some can't be seen with the human eye), and its telescope can see objects only 0.04 in (0.1 cm) wide from 33 ft (10 m) away.

POLAR
ICE CAPS

At the top and bottom of Mars are north and south poles, just like on Earth. The poles are the coldest areas of Mars, as they don't get as much sunlight as the rest of the planet. There is a lot of ice at the poles in areas called ice caps. Mars's ice caps are mostly made of frozen water, but they also contain frozen carbon dioxide from Mars's atmosphere, which is even colder than frozen water. In martian winter, it gets so cold that it snows carbon dioxide, which falls in icy flakes a bit like normal snow. It falls on top of the ice caps and makes them even bigger.

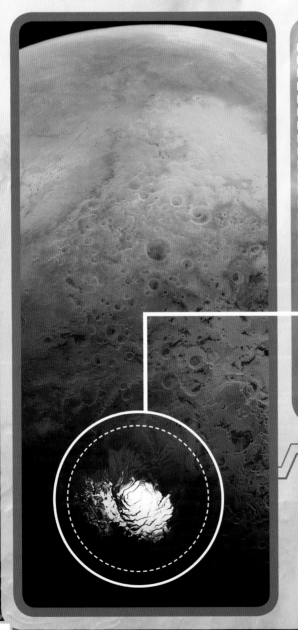

POSITION ON MARS

Mars's south polar cap, which you can see in these images, is about three times smaller than the northern one. It is surrounded by craters and mountains. The north cap features amazing spiraling valleys. Both ice caps have layers of frozen water, frozen carbon dioxide, and dust from martian storms.

SMALL VISITS TO A BIG PLACE

Each robot we send to Mars's surface can only see tiny areas of the planet. We have still only explored less than two percent of its surface.

Orbiting spacecraft have studied Mars in a lot of detail from a distance, but they still don't tell us everything there is to know about the planet. We have to try to figure out what the whole of Mars is like from just the few places that spacecraft have landed! This is a bit like trying to learn about an entire mountain on Earth by looking at just one rock. Because we only get to visit a few places on Mars, we have to choose those places very carefully to make sure we get as much information as possible.

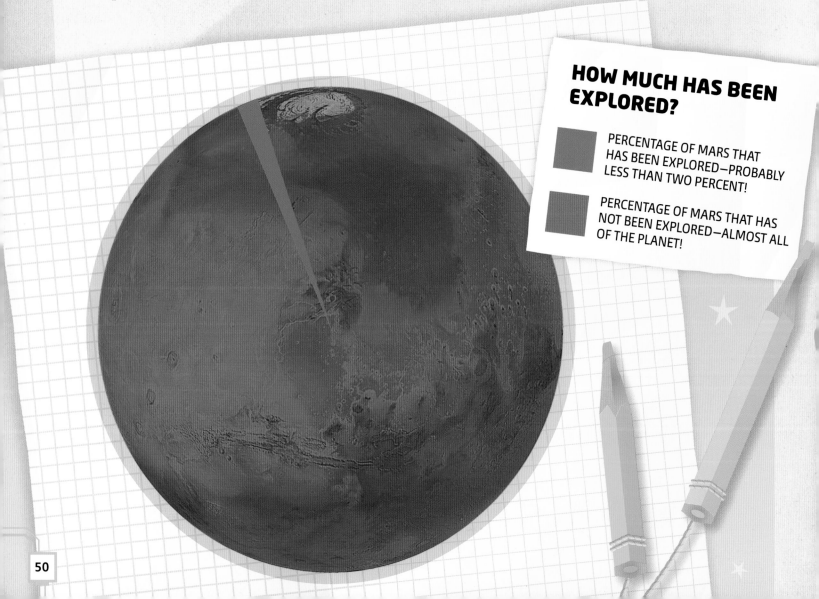

HOW MUCH HAS BEEN EXPLORED?

PERCENTAGE OF MARS THAT HAS BEEN EXPLORED—PROBABLY LESS THAN TWO PERCENT!

PERCENTAGE OF MARS THAT HAS NOT BEEN EXPLORED—ALMOST ALL OF THE PLANET!

RECONNAISSANCE ORBITER

DISH RADIO ANTENNA

SOLAR PANELS

RADAR

CAMERA

WHAT DO WE KNOW?

We know some facts about the places on Mars where spacecraft have already been. But we don't know about the land between these places. Is it the same or different from the places we have explored? Where would you send the next mission? Spacecraft such as the Reconnaissance Orbiter (pages 52–53) get information about Mars from the air to add to our scientific picture of the planet so we can plan where to go next.

LANDING SITE VOTE

COULD THIS SPOT HAVE HAD WATER?

DO WE THINK IT COULD HAVE HELD LIFE?

DOES THIS SITE HAVE LOTS OF ROCKS?

DOES IT HAVE A FLAT AREA NEARBY?

WOULD A SPACECRAFT BE ABLE TO LAND?

IS THIS INTERESTING TO PEOPLE ON EARTH?

WHERE TO LAND?

When choosing a place for a spacecraft to land, scientists have to make sure the ground is flat enough to land on. They often choose a spot that they think could have had water, since this may have also been home to life. The most interesting places have lots of rocks, which contain information about Mars's history. Rocky places are hard to land on, so the best landing sites are flat areas near mountains or cliffs. Committees of people gather information, discuss, and vote on possible sites.

RECONNAISSANCE ORBITER

There have been several orbiters sent to circle Mars, but the one that has sent back the most beautiful images is probably NASA's Mars Reconnaissance Orbiter (MRO).

The orbiter arrived at Mars in 2006, and it orbits at an average height of about 176 miles (283 km) above the surface. Its flight path is programmed so that it will eventually pass over almost every part of Mars. MRO uses a variety of cameras and sensors to build up our most detailed view yet of the Red Planet's wonderful landscape. Some of the most beautiful images we have of Mars were taken by MRO.

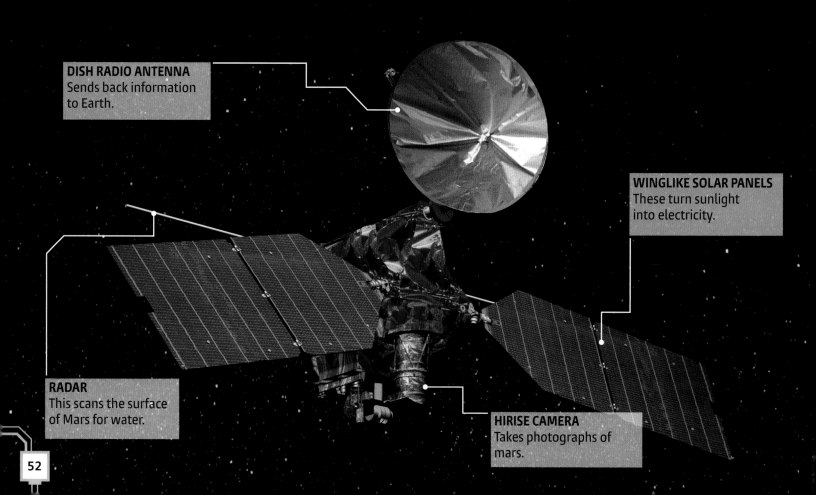

DISH RADIO ANTENNA
Sends back information to Earth.

WINGLIKE SOLAR PANELS
These turn sunlight into electricity.

RADAR
This scans the surface of Mars for water.

HIRISE CAMERA
Takes photographs of mars.

SPECTACULAR SPACE!

ORBITING PHOTOGRAPHER

The most detailed of MRO's cameras, known as HiRISE, looks at Mars through a large telescope. It can pick out details just 1 ft (0.3 m) across. The camera views the landscape in different lights and also in infrared (heat) radiation, which helps scientists identify the minerals in martian rocks and dust.

SNOW-COVERED SAND DUNES

DUNES AND RIPPLES IN A CRATER

A FRESHLY MADE CRATER

A LANDSLIDE DOWN A CLIFF EDGE

LAYERS OF ROCK IN A DRIED-UP RIVER

DARK TRAILS IN THE DUST LEFT BY A STORM

COLORFUL HILLS IN A CANYON

03.

THE FUTURE:

"WILL HUMANS EVER LIVE ON MARS...?"

This city on Mars isn't real—it has been imagined. What do you think a city on Mars could look like many years into the future?

DESTINATION MARS

Scientists have been dreaming about putting humans on Mars for many years. In the next 20 years, it could finally become a reality.

Spacecraft flying around Mars and robots exploring on its surface have told us huge amounts about the planet. Humans, however, want to travel there to explore in person and figure out how we could live there. People can also do many things that robots can't, such as accessing hard-to-reach areas, carrying out experiments, and making decisions based on what they see around them. Getting people to Mars is pretty hard, though. Here are some of the things we need to think about before sending astronauts to the Red Planet.

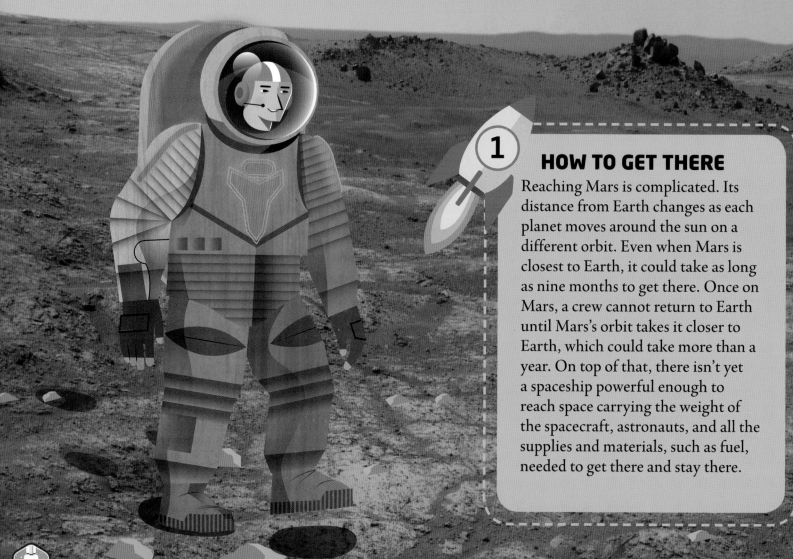

1 HOW TO GET THERE

Reaching Mars is complicated. Its distance from Earth changes as each planet moves around the sun on a different orbit. Even when Mars is closest to Earth, it could take as long as nine months to get there. Once on Mars, a crew cannot return to Earth until Mars's orbit takes it closer to Earth, which could take more than a year. On top of that, there isn't yet a spaceship powerful enough to reach space carrying the weight of the spacecraft, astronauts, and all the supplies and materials, such as fuel, needed to get there and stay there.

2 WHERE TO LIVE

Any buildings on Mars will need to be airtight, to protect the people inside from the thin, toxic martian air. They will also need to protect against extreme temperatures and radiation on Mars. Scientists and designers need to think creatively to find ways to make buildings that do this. Some engineers have even suggested building houses inside caves on Mars.

3 HOW TO GET WATER

Mars is so far away that astronauts couldn't carry all the water that they will need for a long-term mission with them in a spacecraft. Instead, they could get water from ice under the surface of Mars, warming it up to melt it. This water can be used to create oxygen for breathing, and even to make rocket fuel for continued exploration.

4 HOW TO GET AROUND

Once on Mars, astronauts will have plenty of work to do. They will rely on tough, flexible space suits to protect them outside on Mars when exploring. It is sometimes easy to forget how big Mars is, stretching for thousands of miles beyond each landing site. Wheeled vehicles, perhaps with cabins to sleep in, will make longer exploration trips possible.

SOLAR PANELS

Large wings are made up of solar panels that transform sunlight into electricity to be used on the spacecraft. The wings are about 23 ft (7 m) long and provide enough electricity to power 24 three-bedroom houses. They fold up to fit inside the rocket during launch, then open up and face the sun once the spacecraft is in orbit.

ENGINE

The engine on the service module can push the spacecraft toward Mars and back to Earth again. It will help Orion reach speeds of more than 20,000 mph (32,180 kph) as it flies deep into space.

HOW DO WE GET TO MARS?

Imagine packing for a journey that is seven months long and covers about 50 million miles (80 million kilometers)....
That's how far it is to Mars!

Figuring out how to get humans to Mars is a challenge. The spacecraft that carries them must be able to keep the crew safe, and it must be small enough to fit on the rocket that will launch it from Earth. Scientists are working on ideas for spacecraft that can do both of these things. Before it can fly with a crew, a vehicle must first be tested in outer space by itself. This checks the system for safety and shows the design team which parts need to be changed.

ORION SPACECRAFT

This picture shows a design for the Orion spacecraft, a vehicle from ESA and NASA that can transport humans to and from space. Scientists are hoping to use it for flights to Mars in the future. It will carry the crew into orbit, release a lander to put them on Mars, support their missions, then return them to Earth. Orion has two main parts: a capsule, where the crew will live and work, and a service module with the parts that keep the crew alive and the spacecraft working. Advanced computers control Orion. They can give 480 million instructions per second—more than a math teacher could make in a lifetime.

SERVICE MODULE

The service module attaches to the crew module. It holds important equipment to keep the crew alive, such as water tanks and a supply of oxygen.

CREW MODULE

The crew module is cone-shaped and about the size of two large cars. Between four and six astronauts will work, eat, exercise, and sleep in this one-room cabin for months or years on a mission to Mars.

The module also needs to protect the crew inside from the incredibly hot temperatures of about 3,000°F (1,649°C), which it will reach on the outside when it reenters the Earth's atmosphere.

A CHALLENGING JOURNEY

A trip to Mars will be an extremely difficult mental and physical challenge for the people who take it on.

At least nine months of space travel and as many as 500 days on Mars will be hard. If anything goes wrong, help on Earth is very far away — astronauts will only have each other. Research carried out on astronauts who have stayed on space stations for more than a year may help solve some of the problems of living in space, but not all of them. For this reason, people who want to be Mars astronauts must go through many tests on Earth to check the toughness of their bodies and minds.

CREW MODULE

This is an example of the capsule attached to a spacecraft where the crew will travel to Mars. It is so small that the crew will barely be able to stand up inside. Imagine not being able to walk around for nine months!

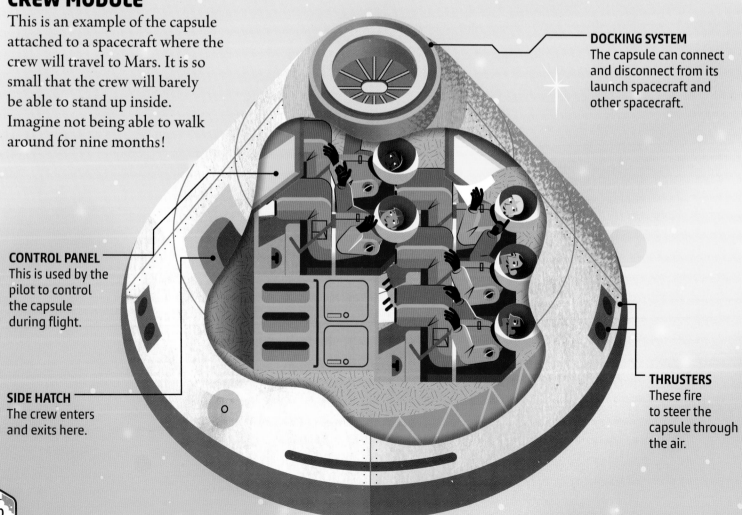

DOCKING SYSTEM
The capsule can connect and disconnect from its launch spacecraft and other spacecraft.

CONTROL PANEL
This is used by the pilot to control the capsule during flight.

SIDE HATCH
The crew enters and exits here.

THRUSTERS
These fire to steer the capsule through the air.

BODY IN SPACE

The main thing affecting an astronaut's body in space is the lack of gravity.
A human body is designed to work with Earth's gravity pulling down on it,
so in space, where gravity is weak, the body doesn't work in the same way.

SPACE SICKNESS

An astronaut's body will have to adjust to the difference in gravity between Earth and Mars. Moving from one field of gravity to another is tough on the body. You would feel sick, just like you might during a car trip.

PUFFY FACE AND SKINNY LEGS

The heart pumps blood up the body. In space, there isn't enough gravity to pull it down the body so that it spreads evenly. As a result, blood gathers in the face, making it puffy, and there isn't enough in the legs, which become thin.

MUSCLE WEAKNESS

For most of the voyage, astronauts are weightless. With no downward pull of gravity to push against, bones and muscles (including the heart) will get weaker. Regular exercise on special machines can help to prevent this.

UNKNOWN FACTORS

No one has been to Mars, so we don't know how being there will affect the human body. Astronauts on Mars will be exposed to radiation and particles from outer space, which may change the body in ways we don't yet know about.

MIND IN SPACE

Spending years in a cramped and isolated spacecraft cabin, facing constant danger,
and being millions of miles from home is sure to test even the most level-headed of minds.

CREWMATES

The crew on board a spacecraft to Mars will have no more than about six people. Space agencies have to select people they believe will get along, thinking about whether they are outgoing or quiet, and if they can speak the same language.

STRESS IN A SMALL SPACE

During their journey to Mars, astronauts will be in a very small capsule, unable to move around very much. They will have to stay focused and positive.

BORED AND TIRED

The long journey will be very boring, which might make the crew grumpy. They might also get very tired — there are an extra 37 minutes in a Mars day, which could affect their sleep patterns.

A LONG WAY FROM HOME

Mars is about 140 million miles (225 million kilometers) from Earth. It could take as long as 45 minutes to send a radio message from Mars to Earth, and 45 minutes to get one back. The crew won't be able to have much contact with their friends and families.

LIVING ON MARS

The best building material for a home on Mars could be a surprising one — ice!

To be able to live on Mars, humans will need homes that can protect them from extreme temperatures, dangerous radiation, and powerful dust storms. NASA scientists and other experts have come up with a brilliant solution — use the ice that lies under the surface of Mars to build houses. They have created concept designs for a dome-shaped building that has a thick shell of ice to protect against tough weather. Inside the shell is a large inflatable structure where humans could live. There is plenty of space for a kitchen, bedrooms, a lab, greenhouse, and more! This is still just a concept design on paper, but it is exciting to think that it could one day become real.

SURVIVAL AIRLOCK

Humans could not survive outside on Mars without a space suit because there is not enough oxygen in the air for them to breathe. A thin atmosphere means that liquids boil at far colder temperatures than on Earth, so a human's blood would boil if they went outside without a suit. In the airlock, astronauts could put their suits on and take them off without being exposed to the dangers outside.

KEEPING WARM

A layer of carbon dioxide between the living area and the ice layer insulates (prevents heat from leaving) the home, keeping it warm inside. Carbon dioxide makes up 96 percent of the thin atmosphere on Mars, so it will not have to be transported all the way from Earth.

PROTECTIVE ICE SHELL

Thick ice makes the perfect shell for a martian home. Underground water can be pumped into the outside of the house and frozen to form a strong shell, as explained below. The ice will let sunlight into the living area so it doesn't feel like the people inside are living in a cave. It will also shield them from the sun's harmful radiation.

GARDENS ON MARS

Plants are already growing on space stations, in heated greenhouses like the one above. Astronauts sent to Mars will stay for a long time so they will have to grow their own food in a similar way.

AMAZING UNDERGROUND RESOURCES

Spacecraft orbiting Mars have detected ice below the planet's surface. To use the ice above ground, machines will have to drill down, melt the ice with microwaves, and pump the liquid up into the home.

EXPLORING MARS

Astronauts on Mars will want to explore the thousands of miles that lie beyond their base, but they will only be able to walk so far…

They will need a speedy vehicle to cover long distances on Mars. Astronauts on missions to the moon in the 1970s used a four-wheeled buggy called the Lunar Roving Vehicle. They sat on top of it in their space suits to make short drives. Mars astronauts, however, might want to spend days or weeks away from their base. They might also want a place to store and study the rocks and other objects they find on their travels. The solution? Take a mini Mars base with them! NASA has designed a concept car that could explore Mars and act as a laboratory at the same time.

STREAMLINED SHAPE

The sleek, smooth car is shaped to glide through martian storms. Its body sits high off the ground, a bit like a monster truck, so it can drive over large rocks and hills without getting damaged by getting rocks wedged underneath.

DRIVER'S SEAT

The front of the car has seats for a driver, a copilot, and a third crew member. It can still be used to drive around and investigate once the back has been removed to use as a laboratory.

SOLAR PANELS

Panels on the roof and sides transform sunlight into electricity to keep the car's batteries charged and supply power for experiments.

HATCH

Astronauts enter and exit through a hatch on the vehicle.

DETATCHABLE LAB

The back half of the car is a mobile laboratory and workshop. It can disconnect from the car, so experiments can continue while the rest of the car is off exploring.

HOLLOW WHEELS

The vehicle's huge wheels are designed to roll over rocks. The tires are like hollow cages, which allows dust to flow through them, rather than getting stuck in small cracks and weighing the vehicle down.

DIFFICULT DRIVING ON MARS

Driving on Mars involves unique problems. Air-filled tires will not work in the thin atmosphere, and solid wheels would grind to a halt, clogged with fine martian dust. Gas and diesel engines won't work, so any vehicle needs to be powered by electricity. The vehicle will also face a lot of obstacles on the ground, such as sharp rocks and sand dunes. Fortunately, gravity on Mars is so weak that heavy vehicles — NASA's one here weighs about 5,500 lb (2,500 kg) on Earth — will weigh much less on Mars.

DRESSED FOR MARS

If you walked outside on Mars without a space suit, you would be dead in seconds — the air would be sucked from your lungs and the liquids in your body would boil.

To go outside their base to work on Mars, an astronaut will need to wear a space suit — a sort of portable spacecraft. Mars suits will need to be much more flexible than the bulky, stiff suits used by astronauts on space walks. NASA's Z-2 space-suit design, shown here, is an example of how Mars suits might look.

GLOWING EDGES

Glowing lights help astronauts to keep track of each other at night or during dust storms. Different colors and shapes can be used to tell who is who when a crew member's face is hidden.

BUILT-IN HATCH

An astronaut can climb into the suit like they would climb into a spacecraft. The suit can be stored on the outside of a Mars vehicle or base, and a hatch on the back of the suit allows the astronaut to climb in directly. The hatch is then covered by a life-support pack that supplies the suit with oxygen.

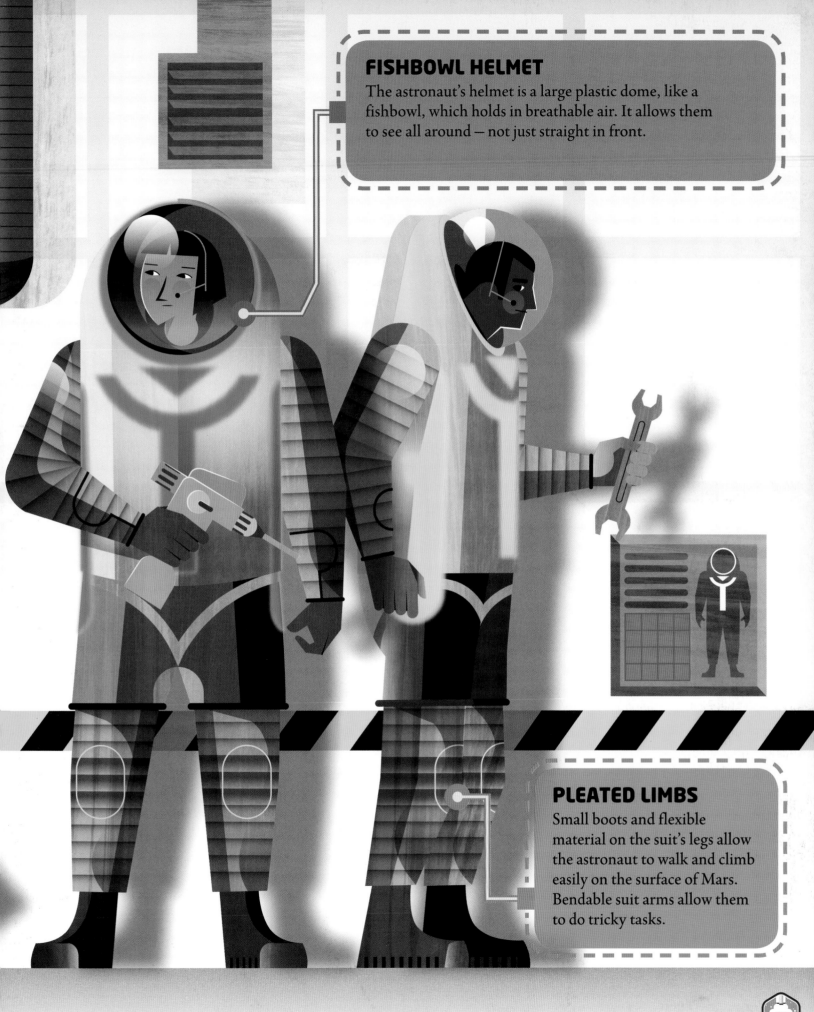

FISHBOWL HELMET

The astronaut's helmet is a large plastic dome, like a fishbowl, which holds in breathable air. It allows them to see all around — not just straight in front.

PLEATED LIMBS

Small boots and flexible material on the suit's legs allow the astronaut to walk and climb easily on the surface of Mars. Bendable suit arms allow them to do tricky tasks.

A NEW GENERATION

It's not all about humans going to Mars. Robotic rovers are getting better and better, and new generations of rovers continue to discover more about the planet.

ExoMars, a joint project between ESA and the Russian State Space Corporation, also known as Roscosmos, is hoping to find the building blocks of life on Mars. Their rover is called Rosalind Franklin, named after the scientist who helped to discover the structure of DNA. NASA also plans to make new discoveries with its rover, which is an upgrade of Curiosity. One of its jobs is to collect rock samples, which will be brought back to Earth by a follow-up robotic mission. China's space agency (China National Space Administration) also hopes to send an orbiter, lander, and rover to Mars.

ROSALIND FRANKLIN

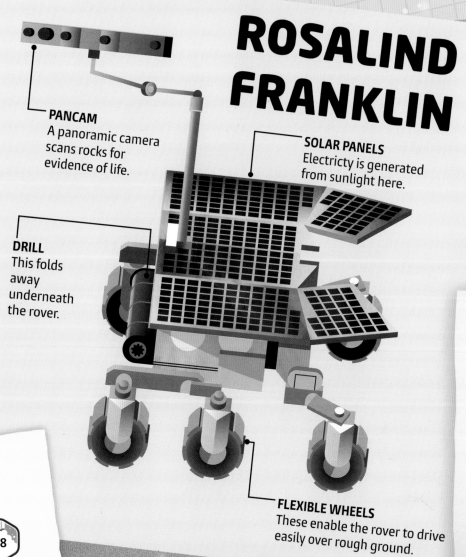

PANCAM
A panoramic camera scans rocks for evidence of life.

SOLAR PANELS
Electricty is generated from sunlight here.

DRILL
This folds away underneath the rover.

FLEXIBLE WHEELS
These enable the rover to drive easily over rough ground.

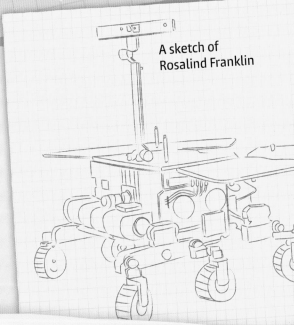

A sketch of Rosalind Franklin

Space agency: ExoMars (ESA and Roscosmos)
Mission goals: Create maps of the ground underneath the landing site; search for water and ice in martian soil; try to find signs of past martian life.

NASA'S ROVER

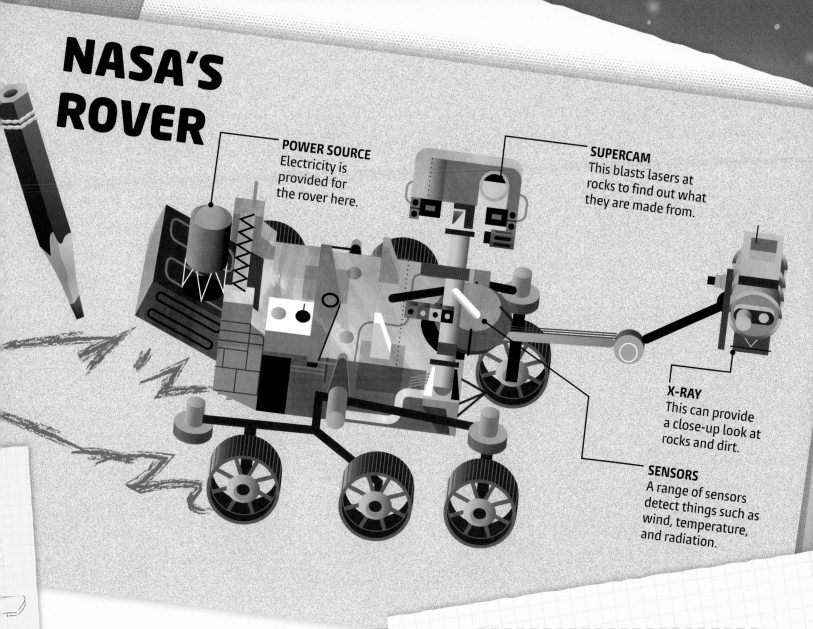

POWER SOURCE
Electricity is provided for the rover here.

SUPERCAM
This blasts lasers at rocks to find out what they are made from.

X-RAY
This can provide a close-up look at rocks and dirt.

SENSORS
A range of sensors detect things such as wind, temperature, and radiation.

Space agency: NASA
Mission goals: Hunt for evidence of ancient life; prepare samples for retrieval by a future robot mission; test technology for future crewed landings.

WHY MORE ROBOTS?

Despite plans for human missions to Mars, rovers still have a key role to play. Not only do they help us to explore as much of Mars as possible, but they can also lay the groundwork for human missions. They are good explorers that are cheaper than humans, and sending robots means human lives aren't put at risk.

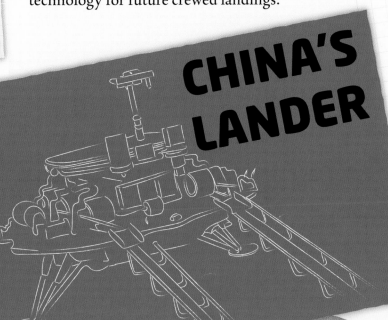

CHINA'S LANDER

Space agency: China National Space Administration
Mission goals: Take photos from orbit; use laser to see under the surface of Mars; search for methane to collect evidence of living things on Mars.

KEEPING MARS CLEAN

Have you ever thought about what kind of bacteria and other germs a spacecraft might be carrying from Earth?

When we send a spacecraft to Mars, it's important to make sure it isn't going to take anything with it that could pollute the planet. It is possible that microorganisms (microscopic living things) could survive on a spacecraft traveling from Earth and end up living on Mars. Then if we were to spot life on Mars, we wouldn't know if we took it or if it was already there. To make sure this doesn't happen, the spacecraft is built in an area known as a clean room. This room is spotlessly clean, a bit like an operating room in a hospital.

BRIGHT, SHINY WALLS

The clean room is kept very dry, so that there is no water for bacteria to feed on. The walls are painted white so that any dirt can be easily spotted. A smooth, shiny surface makes walls easy to wash.

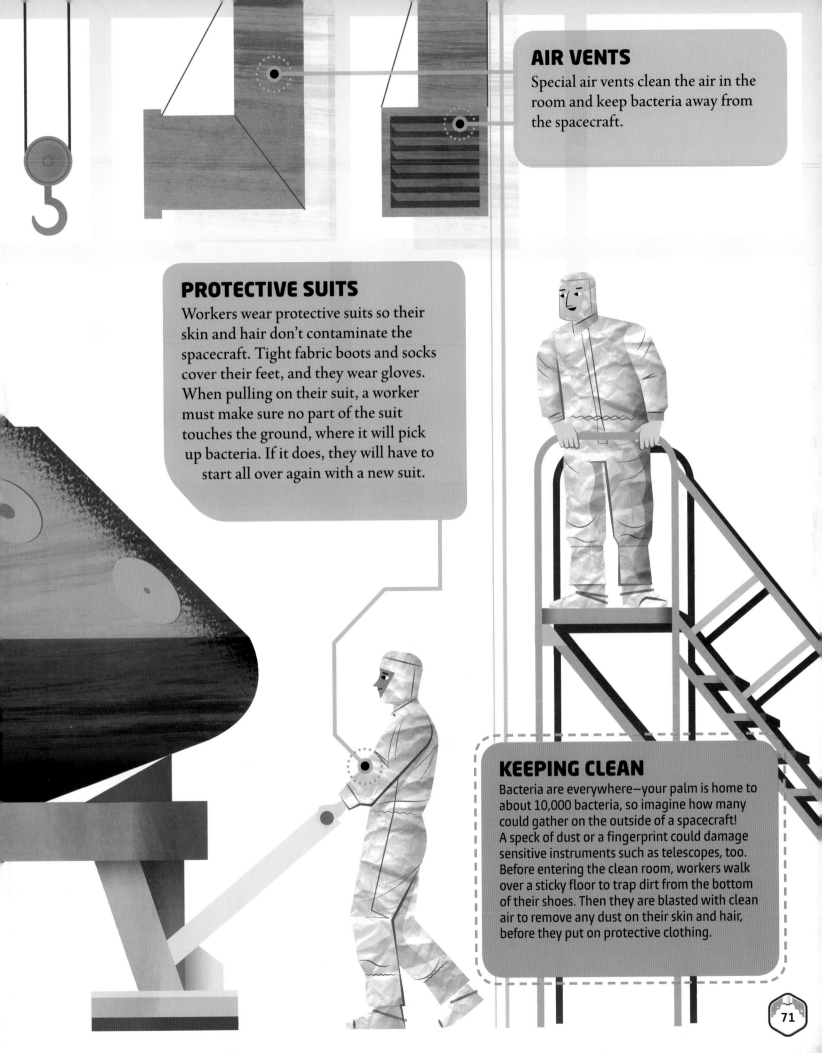

AIR VENTS

Special air vents clean the air in the room and keep bacteria away from the spacecraft.

PROTECTIVE SUITS

Workers wear protective suits so their skin and hair don't contaminate the spacecraft. Tight fabric boots and socks cover their feet, and they wear gloves. When pulling on their suit, a worker must make sure no part of the suit touches the ground, where it will pick up bacteria. If it does, they will have to start all over again with a new suit.

KEEPING CLEAN

Bacteria are everywhere—your palm is home to about 10,000 bacteria, so imagine how many could gather on the outside of a spacecraft! A speck of dust or a fingerprint could damage sensitive instruments such as telescopes, too. Before entering the clean room, workers walk over a sticky floor to trap dirt from the bottom of their shoes. Then they are blasted with clean air to remove any dust on their skin and hair, before they put on protective clothing.

PEOPLE BEHIND THE MISSIONS

Only a few astronauts will actually go to Mars, but it takes hard work from thousands of people on the ground to make a mission possible.

Lots of people with a wide range of skills are needed to send missions to Mars. A mission is so much more than the astronauts or spacecraft that go to space. There are hundreds of jobs that need to be done that you might not have even considered. Before launch, everything needs to be planned down to the finest detail. During the mission, crew on the ground need to be on hand day and night in case of problems. And even when astronauts or spacecrafts have returned to Earth, the work has barely started. Scientists then have to look at the information collected on Mars to learn more about its history, and this research could take years!

Here are just a few of the many jobs that need to be done for a mission.

SUIT DESIGNER

Astronauts need space suits to protect against radiation, heat, and cold. Suit designers create suits that do this, sometimes even inventing new materials. They test their designs, seeing if anything needs to be changed. Designers are creative and like solving problems.

ENGINEER

All equipment for a mission has to be designed and built by engineers. Each piece must be small and light to fit inside the spacecraft, and easy to repair during the mission. Engineers work well in a team and keep trying without giving up.

GRAPHIC DESIGNER

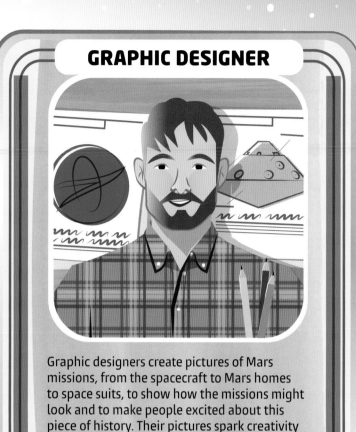

Graphic designers create pictures of Mars missions, from the spacecraft to Mars homes to space suits, to show how the missions might look and to make people excited about this piece of history. Their pictures spark creativity and wonder about space.

COMPUTER ENGINEER

Computers are essential to any space mission, from guiding a spacecraft in to land to making sure astronauts have enough food. Computer engineers use coding to do these things. They plan for any possible problems and make sure that solutions are built into the codes.

DIETICIAN

Astronauts' meals on a Mars mission will have to last for the whole trip. Dieticians must create food that can be eaten while floating in the spaceship. Astronauts' bodies will change in space, so the food has to provide nutrients to help them stay strong and healthy.

PSYCHOLOGIST

It is hard to predict how a crew will get along on a Mars mission. They will share a very small space for a long time and will get frustrated, bored, and homesick. Psychologists teach astronauts how to manage their feelings and help each other when they feel upset.

WHO WILL GO TO MARS?

Would you like to travel to Mars? Read on to find out what skills you would need.

Mars astronauts will study the rocks, soil, and weather and look for signs of past and present life. They will spend a lot of time with other people, so they must be able to work well in a team. A lot of what they will be doing on Mars will never have been done before, so they must be good at using their imaginations to solve problems. A trip to Mars should be taken very seriously — scientists don't know how astronauts' bodies will be affected by living on another planet.

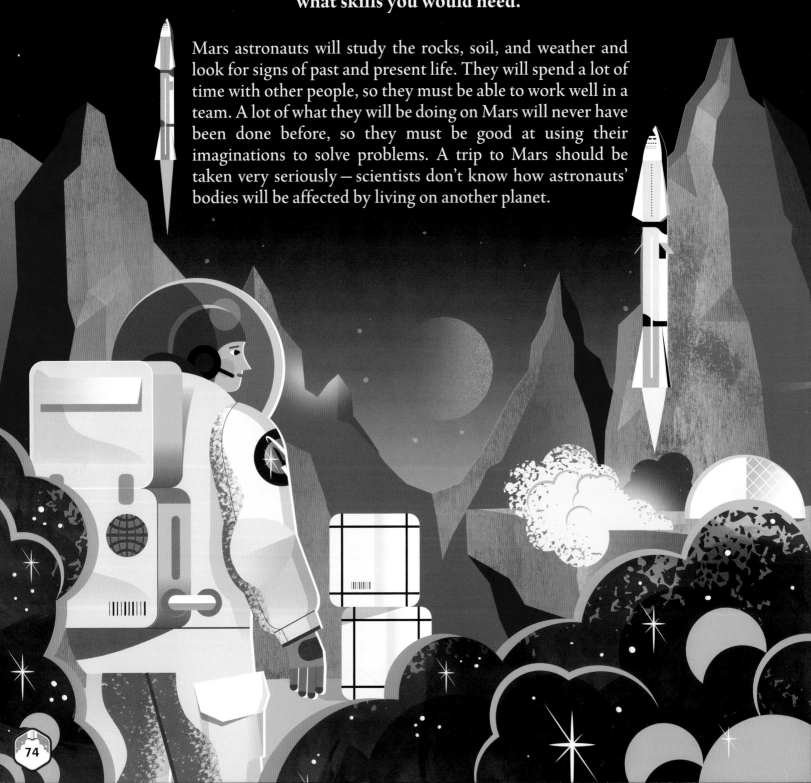

HAVE YOU GOT WHAT IT TAKES?

IF YOU DREAM OF GOING TO MARS, THE BEST THING TO DO IS FIND SOMETHING YOU LOVE AND GET BETTER AT IT.

Sometimes that something will get you selected to become an astronaut. But if it doesn't, you will be doing something that makes you happy. Thousands of people have applied to go to space, but only a few hundred people have ever been selected. They had many different jobs before becoming astronauts, from pilots and scientists to doctors and teachers. But they were all dedicated to doing their jobs well, learning every day, and trying again when things didn't work out.

A FEW SKILLS THAT MARS ASTRONAUTS NEED:

IS A TEAM PLAYER
Can you listen to others and work together to find a solution to a problem, even if you disagree?

DOESN'T GIVE UP
Will you keep trying when something is frustrating or difficult? On Mars, you might be the only person who can complete a task.

LOVES MATH AND SCIENCE
Do you enjoy math and science, especially geology? These subjects are useful for studying the rocks, soil, and weather on Mars.

IS COMFORTABLE IN SMALL SPACES
Would you be comfortable spending a long time in a small space? To get to Mars, you will have to travel in a small spacecraft for up to two years.

DOESN'T SHOW OFF
Do you care more about the goal of the mission and doing a good job than about being famous?

AND MOST IMPORTANT... LOVES MARS!
Are you curious about the universe? Do you spend time learning new things and practicing new skills? To go to Mars, you will need to be interested in it!

WHAT'S NEXT?

There are still hundreds of questions left to answer about Mars, and so much more of the planet to explore.

The successful orbiters, landers, and rovers we have sent to Mars may have revealed many of the planet's amazing secrets, but there are still a lot of things we don't know. Was Mars really covered in oceans? Did ancient life survive there billions of years ago? Could it still be surviving today?

Each new mission adds a little bit more to our picture, but the fact that there are so many unknown things about Mars is a big part of why so many people want to go there. The future holds many exciting journeys into space to try to solve some of the mysteries of the incredible Red Planet.

METHANE MYSTERY

A small amount of a gas called methane occasionally appears in the atmosphere of Mars, although it disappears quickly. On Earth, methane is usually released by volcanoes or living things. Scientists are wondering if methane on Mars is evidence that active volcanoes or even living things still survive there.

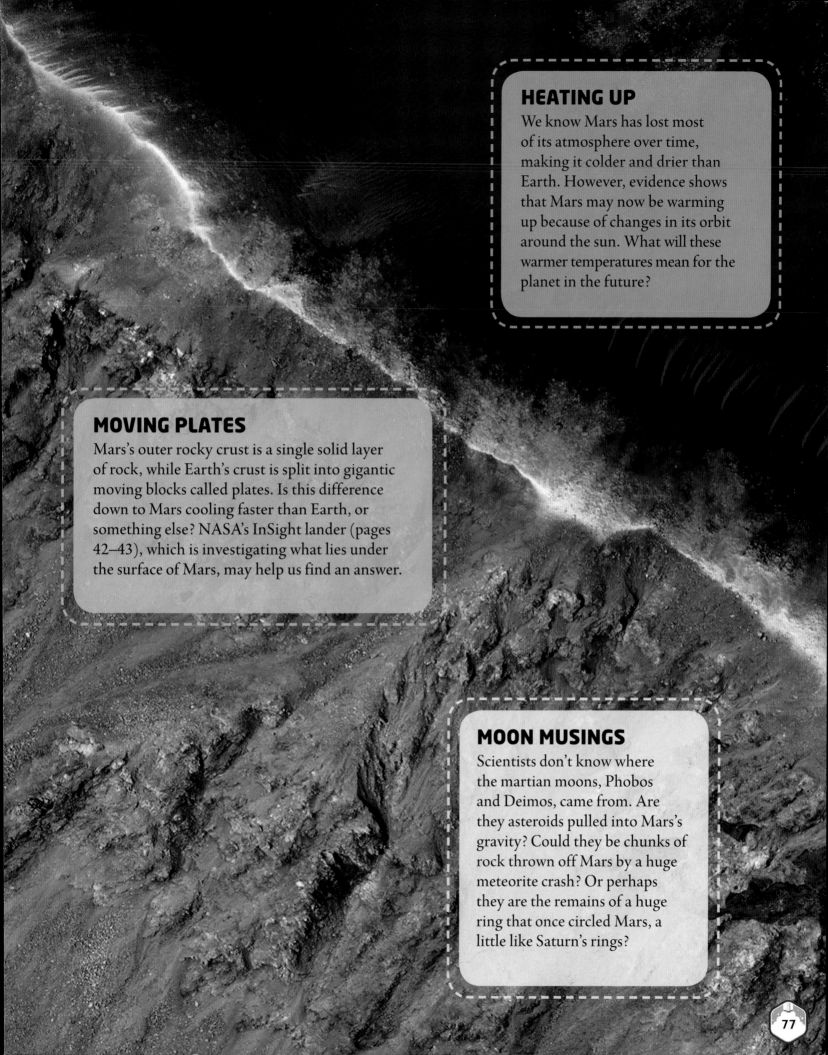

HEATING UP

We know Mars has lost most of its atmosphere over time, making it colder and drier than Earth. However, evidence shows that Mars may now be warming up because of changes in its orbit around the sun. What will these warmer temperatures mean for the planet in the future?

MOVING PLATES

Mars's outer rocky crust is a single solid layer of rock, while Earth's crust is split into gigantic moving blocks called plates. Is this difference down to Mars cooling faster than Earth, or something else? NASA's InSight lander (pages 42–43), which is investigating what lies under the surface of Mars, may help us find an answer.

MOON MUSINGS

Scientists don't know where the martian moons, Phobos and Deimos, came from. Are they asteroids pulled into Mars's gravity? Could they be chunks of rock thrown off Mars by a huge meteorite crash? Or perhaps they are the remains of a huge ring that once circled Mars, a little like Saturn's rings?

GLOSSARY

ACIDIC
Made from acid, a sour substance

AIRLOCK
Small, sealed room used to enter or exit a spacecraft or building

ANTENNA
A device that picks up or sends out radio waves

ASTEROID
Rocky object that travels around the sun

ASTRONAUT
Person who travels into space

ASTRONOMER
Type of scientist who studies space

BACTERIA
Tiny living thing

CAPSULE
Small compartment or vehicle for space flight

CLIMATE
Average weather conditions of an area

CONCEPT
Idea for a design that hasn't been made in real life yet

CORE
Center of a planet

CRATER
Dip in the surface of a planet caused by an object, such as a meteorite, crashing into it

CRUST
Rocky outer part of a planet

DECELERATION
Slowing down

ENTRY
When a spacecraft moves from outer space into the atmosphere of a planet

EQUATOR
Imaginary line that runs horizontally through the middle of a planet

ERUPTION
When lava, gas, or ash explodes out of a volcano

GALAXY
A collection of stars, dust, gas, and space held together by gravity

GEOLOGY
Study of the ground and rocks on planets

HABITABLE ZONE
Area that is the right temperature to live in

HATCH
Small door

IRON
Type of metal

LABORATORY
Place for scientific experiments or study

LANDER
Spacecraft designed to land on a moon or a planet

LASER
Narrow beam of powerful light

LAVA
Melted rock that comes from a volcano or a crack in the surface of a planet

MARSQUAKE
Shaking in the ground on Mars, like an earthquake on Earth

METEORITE
Piece of rock from space that comes through Earth's atmosphere and lands on its surface

METHANE
Type of gas

MICROSCOPIC
Too small to see without a microscope

MILKY WAY
Galaxy we live in

MOLTEN
Melted

ORBITER
Spacecraft designed to fly around a moon or planet without landing on it

POLAR
To do with the poles of a planet

RADAR
Technology that detects faraway objects by sending out radio waves, which bounce off the object back to the radar

RADIATION
Energy that travels through space in waves or particles

REENTRY
When a spacecraft moves from outer space into Earth's atmosphere when returning to Earth from space

ROVER
Vehicle that drives on the surface of a moon or planet that is not Earth

SATELLITE
Space object designed to orbit planets or moons

SEISMOMETER
Instrument that measures the movements of the ground

SENSOR
Technology that senses and measures things such as movement, sound, heat, or light.

SOLAR PANEL
Surface that creates electricity from the energy in sunlight

SPACECRAFT
Vehicle that travels in space

STAR
Huge, glowing sphere of gas, such as the sun

TELESCOPE
Tool used to look at objects very far away

UNIVERSE
The whole of space

INDEX

ACKNOWLEDGMENTS

DK would like to thank Becky Walsh for proofreading and Marie Lorimer for the index.

The publisher would like to thank the following for their kind permission to reproduce their photographs:
(Key: a-above; b-below/bottom; c-center; f-far; l-left; r-right; t-top)
8 NASA: JPL / USGS (b). **9 Fotolia:** dundanim (t). **10-11 Alamy Stock Photo:** Bruce Rolff (b). **11 NASA:** JPL-Caltech / MSSS (tl, cla, cra). **16 Dreamstime.com:** Itechno (br).
16-17 NASA: (tc). **17 iStockphoto.com:** Photos.com (cla). **20-21 ESA / Hubble:** DLR / FU Berlin,CC BY-SA 3.0 IGO (Highlands). **22 NASA:** (b). **23 Alamy Stock Photo:** NASA
Image Collection (cla). **26-27 Alamy Stock Photo:** Stocktrek Images, Inc.. **27 NASA:** Goddard Space Flight Center (tl). **28-29 ESO:** P. Horálek. **32-33 Alamy Stock Photo:**
Science Photo Library. **38-39 ESA / Hubble:** DLR / FU Berlin (G. Neukum). **38 NASA:** JPL / USGS (cla); JPL-Caltech / USGS (ca); NASA's Earth Observatory (cl). **40-41 Alamy
Stock Photo:** Stocktrek Images, Inc.. **41 Fotolia:** dundanim (cra/Earth). NASA: JPL (ca); JPL / MSSS (cra). **43 NASA:** JPL-Caltech (tl, cr, br). **44-45 NASA:** JPL-Caltech / Univ. of
Arizona. **45 NASA:** JPL-Caltech / UA (crb). **46 Alamy Stock Photo:** Nerthuz (b). **46-47 NASA:** JPL-Caltech. **48 ESA / Hubble:** DLR / FU Berlin, CC BY-SA 3.0 IGO (bl). **48-49 ESA /
Hubble:** DLR / FU Berlin / Bill Dunford. **50 NASA:** JPL / USGS (b). **52 NASA:** (b). **53 NASA:** (cr, bl); JPL-Caltech / University of Arizona (cl, clb); JPL-Caltech / Univ. of Arizona (tr,
crb, br). **56-57 Alamy Stock Photo:** Jürgen Fälchle. **58-59 ESA / Hubble.** **62-63 NASA:** JPL-Caltech / MSSS. **63 NASA:** (tr). 64-65 NASA: Kim Shiflett. **66 NASA:** Bill Stafford (bl).
76-77 NASA: JPL-Caltech / Univ. of Arizona
Cover images: Front: **NASA:** JPL-Caltech c; Back: **Alamy Stock Photo:** Nerthuz br; Spine: **NASA:** JPL-Caltech t

All other images © Dorling Kindersley
For further information see: www.dkimages.com